Pathway to Awakening your Seventh Soul

Ahmed Y. Tatieta

Tatieta Book Publishing, LLC

Los Angeles, California

tatietabookpublishing@yahoo.com

www.ahmedtatieta.com

ISBN: 978-1-7346773-7-9 (EBook version)

ISBN: 978-1-7-346773-8-6 (Paperback version)

Limits of Liability and Disclaimer of Warranty

This book is solemnly for those who deem it valuable and informative to their well-being; and for people seeking health, peace and happiness. The purpose of this book is to educate and provide valuable information based on a research. Upon reading so many books and with an understanding, the result is in your hands. The content of the book does not guarantee that anyone following the various technics, suggestions, tips, ideas, or strategies will immediately become concrete and successful in trying to get well, but the truth remains that knowledge is power. This could make room for positive change and a shift of consciousness.

This is a good faith book that independently works on a good faith basis. Knowing that knowledge is power, every sentence read in this book can contribute to a peace of mind.

The author is neither liable nor responsible to anyone with respect to any loss and damages occurred, or any alleged damages caused, or to be caused directly or indirectly, by the use of the information contained in this book. With this in mind, when it comes to health, many subjects and disciplines have to be considered. But, at the end, each individual experience is unique and individually lived. This is not a professional advice or service to you.

Health is a constant maintenance and requires daily care and abnegation. And my advice to you is to never judge a book by its cover. Only the sick need a doctor. We should pray for each other; and the prayer of the righteous one is powerful and more effective. Always remember that God will never leave you behind, nor forsake you. Health is everything; all strength is with God; and to live is to forgive.

Printed in the United States of America.

About the Author

Ahmed Tatieta is an award winning author of three world-wide best-selling books "Soul Pathway to Total Health" and "The Path to a Long and Healthy Life" and "Pathway to Awakening your Seventh Soul". He is a lawyer by formation and founder of a book publishing company called "Tatieta Book Publishing, a limited liability company incorporated in California.

He started writing the self-help books after he himself has fallen sick; he decided then to stop looking for others for his own healing when he realized sooner or later that health had a lot of components to it. Health has a physical component, a mental and spiritual components too; making health something that the patient himself had to actively get involved in his/her own healing process. After couple of years of research about health in general, he realized that the knowledge had to be shared so that his friends and family could also beneficiate from it, as it was a knowledge that was not being taught generally in our modern school system. Besides, by reading his books, you will get the necessary knowledge and understanding in how to alleviate pain, how to make your own medicine, how to properly manage your stress and your time, how to meditate, how to love yourself and others, how to choose a proper diet and why, how to connect to the spirit realm, how to know God, how to manage your money, how to manage your relationships/marriage, how to control your emotions, how to control your mind, how to think without being prejudicial, how to understand the world, how your soul, mind and body are connected, how to read and cleanse your aura, how to balance your chakras, how to practice deep breathing, how to take care of your temple, how to take care of your environment, how to unplug yourself from the matrix and most importantly how to know thyself.

The reason why he invested so many years of research (more than ten years) is to bring to you a general knowledge that everyone has to know no matter who he/she is or no matter how many degrees and certificates he/she has. By doing the research, he realized that the most important thing in life is not the certificates or degrees but to know yourself; which includes having enough knowledge in how to properly assist himself and his family for basic health and nutrition care.

In a way, these are accumulated knowledge and understandings that if society was not just about power and control, everyone should have been taught about these various knowledge before studying anything else. These books are a must read and his contribution was to help and save someone from going through what he went through; specially, he didn't want his own children to have to struggle to get those knowledge and understanding, that are primordial and a condition to live a healthy life. One of his words is "If I don't do it, who-else is going to do it? And besides, who-else is best suited to do a critical research than a trained lawyer." It was a well-deserved and worthy sacrificed to better himself and the next generations with enough wisdom.

In his opinion, those three books comprise a little bit of everything that is a requirement for his friends and family to know. They are the books, he would have looked for, and the next generations and his descendants could simply read them, meditate on the subjects and be able to free their own minds and souls from the shackle and chains of life. There is no more excuse unless you are not made aware of the existence of those three books that are complementary to the circle. You have all you need to know and to be free from the world oppressions included in the books. All you need to do is to put the know-how practically in your life, as you should know by now that knowledge is power. And there is no more power than being able to take good care of yourself and your family physically, mentally and spiritually. Now he understood why, the oppressor had to always take your knowledge away in order to better enslave you and your next of kin.

Because, once a slave gets to know what are in those three books, there is no way, he/she would remain a slave since now totally free from outside bondage and with enough skills, none of his would remain a slave. Resource your minds and spirits with what you were supposed to be taught anyway if your family traditions and lineages were not abruptly disrupted and displaced. Feed your mind and soul with the proper diets and initiative knowledge that your ancestors knew and have always made sure to pass it down from generation to generation. Claim back what is rightfully yours and make a better use of it. Each one teaches one and spread the word. As this is the word of the truth, from the truth, leading to the truth. And you know that by all means, the truth always prevails.

Pathway to Awakening your Seventh Soul

Ahmed Y. Tatieta

Table of Contents

Introduction

The world is old. The world has been here for a very long time. No human on this earth could ever pretend to know how old the world is. Try predicting it yourself to see if you can. All we do is an attempt to give it a number in vain, because it is just not possible. It is said that earth is as old as billions of years. Now when it comes again to how long or when the first Man ever created walked on earth, it is another problem that will remain confusing just as the age of the earth/world. Truly, most of the records have been destroyed, hidden, inexistent or still not discovered yet. One thing that will be true until tomorrow is that someone somewhere is determined with all means necessary that certain truth throughout the world doesn't get to you. The world is so old that I can guarantee you that there have been millions of kings and Queens. Some good ones and some bad ones. Again, the world is so old that I can guarantee you that there have been millions of gods that were worshiped throughout the ages. In fact, I will guarantee you that there is no ground on this earth that has not been a cemetery, a burial place, a war zone;

even the soil you are walking or seating on right now has its own story.

Over the years, people have become so lost spiritually that they all started looking for the face of God outside of God. Or should I say that knowledge was hidden from them for so long that there were nobody that knew better as time went by, not even the old parents.

It is unconceivable that someone eating, pooping and growing already inside God would lack the common sense to know that God is nowhere else but where that person is. Earth is spinning around and yet your face is up looking to see God. If God had a special location, I bet you, you will miss God location because earth always spins. By the time you look up with your prayers, oops you have already missed God.

The name God is just another name on top of millions of other names mankind has given to the entity that he/she doesn't really know. If everybody knew that God was innocently accused of participating in human affairs due to mankind growing ignorance, the world will be one step ahead to peace of minds. That way, we will no longer have someone claiming God as his/her property. "that's my God" "my God is stronger than yours" "my God is the only God" "my God will punish you" "my God will revenge me" "my God is merciful" "everyone shall bow down to my God". In truth, God is no-one's property. Nobody has ever seen God. And nobody knows where God is, besides within us and everywhere that you can think of. We are already living inside God or inside God's property; so how would God be different than what you see? God does not have preferences or giving favors to one group of people in the detriment of another group. God is above any feelings, any emotions, any prejudices, any judgmental faculties, any laws; God is indeed above all Beings and does not have an opposing partner in the name of Satan/devil competing against God, for men/women souls. You alone are responsible for your soul salvation. God does not participates in human worldly affairs because of all the various universal laws God already puts in place. That's God's presence already. You can talk to God all day long, but if the law says you must work for your own bread, believe me, you might die of hunger if you seat and wait to take advantage of someone else's hard labor. Prayers only work within the confinements of God's Laws. Let me use another simple example. Grab you a corn seed and put it under your pillow. Now gather 1000 pastors, 1000 imams, 1000 monks, 1000 animists, 1000 priests and 1000 atheists; tell them all to pray their respective gods for the grain under your pillow to germinate and give fruit. I bet you that no matter how loud they pray and for however long, the corn seed will never grow. Because you have broken the laws of the universe that tell you to put the seed on a fertile ground and to water it for some time, then, only then your seed will grow to a tree/plant and produce a fruit. The same goes with the one seating and just keep praying God to get rid of his/her disease. There are laws and you must know them in order to grow in spirit and health.

God has no favoritism, nor enemies, and nobody can claim to ever have God because God never went nowhere and God is for everyone, not just for you. Therefore, God is here already with you and there is no more need to be looking for God's return since God has never left you anyway.

What is Soul Loss?

"For What Shall It Profit Man, If He Gains The Whole World, And Suffer The Loss of His Soul"? Christ

Soul Loss is a sort of a fragmentation of the inner-body that caused a person suffering from soul loss to remain disconnected from his/her physical, spiritual and emotional bodies in a given time. In most cultures everywhere in the world, soul loss is a true phenomenon that the shamans and spiritual healers all agreed that all illness is linked to a typical loss of the soul in general. Soul loss is also usually caused by any traumatic experience that causes an intense shock to the person's mind and inner-bodies. It is always an unexpected event that surprises the mind of the person, an event that comes with pain and suffering to a point that for the soul to cope and to not feel or share the pain, it has to step out away from the person's mind and body. That's why soul loss is considered an inner fragmentation because the person will lose some of the primary connections with his/her soul's true nature including some connection with his/her mind also once the soul steps away during trauma.

In a simple word, soul loss does not mean that you have lost your full soul. Your soul always belongs to you and will not go anywhere if it will comfort you to know. Soul loss means that you have lost vitality, inner-insight, vital energy and sensitivity. You have lost touch of some parts of your own soul. Soul loss might look like a bad thing, but it really helps the person cope better during intense pain and suffering. Soul loss is needed and necessary for your soul, your psyche or your entire being to cope with pain and it is the only avenue the soul has and knows how to protect you and itself. The soul jumps out to avoid sharing and witnessing an excessive pain inflicting upon you. And in doing so over and over at each imminent threat and the likeliness of experiencing a pain, it causes you the bearer of your soul to suffer what you now know to be "soul loss". And over time it might build up just like any other issue that doesn't get a proper care.

The Causes of Soul Loss

The causes of a soul loss or loss soul are multiple. The most common ones are accidents, breaking one part of the body, fighting in a war, being politically persecuted, running for your dear life, surviving a domestic violence, being wrongfully jailed, incarceration, death of a relative or a friend, forced labor, slavery, colonization, police brutality, false imprisonment, lynching, victim of an earthquake, fire, hurricane, tsunami, and tornados. More causes will be victims of a terror attack, long-term sickness, death of a loved-one and near death experiences. Even surgery, illness, extreme poverty, pandemic, divorce, heart-breaks, intense disappointment, betrayal, heart attacks, unstable relationships, broken relationships, abusive relationships, sexual abuse, rapes, child abuse, molestation, domestic verbal abuse and loss of freedom of movement-speech can be responsible for a soul loss and actually cause any person to lose touch of his/her true nature beyond the silent sufferings, scars and wounds. Any physical, spiritual and emotional upset, verbal abuse or pain that lead to a psychological unbalance could be considered causes of soul loss. I must remind you that soul loss is as in comparison to a loss of vitality, loss of the essence of life, loss of the vital life force that sometimes lead to hopelessness and desolation. It is equal to losing your soulful energy, your mental stability and even a loss of the sense of direction to take in your life.

The Consequences of Soul Loss

The consequences of a soul loss on the person are remarkably noticeable when paid attention. After a soul loss experience, the person will feel empty like missing something or a piece of herself/himself. The person becomes aware that something is missing in his/her life. Most people don't know that what they are looking for as a missing piece to feel whole again is linked to their soul losing vitality and energy to tackle day to day life expectations. During the event of a soul loss, the person loses parts of his/her soul in different places including different spiritual dimensions via dreams, nightmares or near death experiences. Soul loss can also be linked to witchcraft and to the negative effect of the evil eye on someone. What is important for you to know is that the soul parts left the body and carry with them your joy, your gifts, your spiritual gifts, your desires, your peace of mind, your self-esteem, your light, your glow, your creativity, your insights, your ambitions, your mojo, your health, your sensitivity, your empathy, your compassion, your will, your patience, your goals, your inner-sense of direction, your common-sense, your taste for life, your capacity to focus, your self-respect, your imagination, your self-love, your self-worth, your dignity, your grace, your third eye vision, your sixth sense ability, your tolerance level, including your trust level and your vital endurance. Because the soul parts are lost and can no longer find their way back to your body, you will experience a feeling of emptiness or a feeling of not being whole. Imagine how in a single life, how many times have we experience some or all of these consequences of the soul loss described up there upon on our minds, souls and bodies?

The Experiences from Soul Loss

People react and experience soul loss in different ways. But the most shared are when you start wondering what happened to your old you in a negative way; chances are, you are already experiencing a soul loss. Whenever you catch yourself saying how you have become different after a previous event in your life in a negative way, parts of your soul are loss. Basically, what can cause you to suffer a loss soul might differ from another person since it depends on how impactful the situation affected the inner-body to be fragmented. In most cases, when you notice yourself seeking external satisfaction in order to fill up the empty spaces within you, you are experiencing a soul loss. Some people cope while taping into an external source hoping to fill the missing parts of their soul's vital energies dispersed in between worlds and spiritual dimensions.

Signs of Soul Loss and When to Know You are Experiencing a Soul Loss

Signs of soul loss involve a difficulty forgiving, a difficulty being present/focus, immune system deficiency problems, chronic depression, prolonged stress, anxiety, mental health issues, substance abuse, addiction, loneliness, eating disorder, memory gaps, angry for no reason, irritated for any reason, mood swings, suicidal, unapologetic, self-incrimination, lack of self-control, uncontrollable emotions, lack of pity, inconvincible, and insomnia, including difficulty holding a relationship or a need to be in one regardless of the company. In the attempt to fill the void within you and to find what is missing, most people resolve to drinking excessively, living a reckless-careless life, living a fast life, having excessive sex with multiple partners, and the rest of us have developed an ego as a survival mechanism. With the ego, you have forged yourself a new and fake personality that you jealously protect from being discovered by others. Therefore, we have become compulsive liars, ungrateful to life, too much pride, pathological liar and narcissist, coupled with identity disorders, post traumatic disorders, self-incriminatory, mental disorders, self-hate and co-dependent. The missing pieces in your life caused by the soul losing parts of its vital characteristic have pressured you to seek for outside solutions. With the confusion, you end up feeling alienated from your own self, alienated from others and even alienated from your divine self. You the person experiencing signs of soul loss will unintentionally live in fear, in shame, in guilt, in hopelessness, numbness, heartless, and unforgiving to yourself and others. You are experiencing all these signs because you have lost control of your consciousness, of your soul's parts and your source of life and security. That's why you created an ego, a pride, or a multiple alter egos and in a worse-case scenario, you might become suicidal or supper-aggressive with self-destructive behaviors or compulsions.

You might be wondering now what you can do in a case of a soul loss. The solution is the retrieval of all the parts of your soul that are missing in your life because chances are, you might be experiencing a soul loss right now. And frankly, it is an endless battle because every day, a lot of events in our lives might always bring soul loss into our door-steps. No-one is immune to it, not even the healers, priests, pastors, imams and spiritual guiders. It is a constant self-inner work that requires discipline and endurance.

What Can You Do to Cure Soul Loss?

As a result of the soul loss, until you retrieve the missing parts of your soul, you will not be able to live a true healthy life, a true creative life or a life full of happiness and peace. In order to reconnect with your soul, you will need to do inner engineering that consist of practicing mindfulness, meditation, inner work, singing, chanting, dancing, yoga, visualization, breathing control, plant medicine (guided by a knowledgeable herbal specialist), nature immersion and mind/emotions control etc. It is important for you to understand that soul loss does not fix itself. You need to put in work and intent to be successful in retrieving your soul's missing parts to be whole again by getting personally involved. Since the parts of your missing soul cannot find their way back to you by themselves, there is an urgent need for you to be wanting to go through your own journey of retrieving your soul's parts. Inner-engineering is the way and the process might take a little bit longer than you probably anticipated or expected. Because it can takes months, even years to reconnect back all the soul's missing parts that are your vital strength. Imagine a life time of missing soul parts throughout your life and it is clear that you need to take the journey with the knowledge that only you can sustain and maintain your mental, spiritual, physical, emotional, psychological and divine health. This process has nothing to do with your religious appurtenance and beliefs system. It doesn't matter if you are Muslim, Animist, Christian, Buddhist or an unbeliever; every-body experience soul loss as scars and wounds in our lives. And those silent scars and wounds are not going to fix and healed merely by themselves. You need to participate and understand that health is a constant maintenance. If it is your first time hearing about soul loss or having it break down in writing for your understanding, remain open-minded because we all learn something new every day and apparently it is for sure that you don't know everything either. This exercise of retrieving the parts of your soul that are missing have nothing to do with religion and you should not be a fool to think otherwise. Your stomach ache doesn't care if you believe in God or not; nor is your loss of self-worth. It is your duty to care and heal your own temple (body, mind and soul); but sometimes we need knowledge to rescue us from perishing and since you don't want to perish, stay open-minded when it comes to knowledge. Soul loss doesn't care whether you are saved or a born again Christian just like diabetes and corona-virus didn't. You can also seek the help of a specialist when needed.

Soul Retrieval with the Help of a Professional

Instead, if you don't think that you are up to undertaking your own soul's parts retrieval, you can always hire or seek the help of a shaman, a spiritual healer, a soul doctor or a professional soul's retriever. Some real pastors, imams and ministers can be helpful as long as they are not just telling you to pray about it and have faith without putting in some work. Even with the help of a professional, you will still need to maintain consistently your health after being healed. Remember that it is just like going to your regular doctor or physician, but even though, you still have to watch your diet, your thinking, your emotions, your whole life style in order to keep your optimal health.

The view of soul loss in shamanism is when the soul while traveling to other realms or spiritual dimensions, often time and most likely, the soul gets possessed by spirits. In the process of your soul rubbing against a different entity of beings via possession, parts of the soul stay there in those spiritual realms. The retrieval of the said soul from possession is to recover all the parts of the soul in order for the person to be whole again, thereby finding inner peace and completion as a full being. Each time that your soul gets possessed, a little bit of your soul gets left behind and has to be recovered. You may then have parts of your psyche or in some cases the entire aspects of the psyches totally blocked out or unintentionally repressed. In a situation of a trauma, the missing part of your soul might not even be aware that the trauma that caused it to step out of your body is over; and that it is now safe to come back. Instead, that part of your soul is still out there wandering and hurting; living his/her own life. In some cases of soul's retrieval, the part of the missing soul might be even reluctant to come back due to the fact that the missing part is not even aware of the dissociation, or simply just don't want to return back to the body. And when a successful retrieval happens in most cases, the soul's part comes back again with all the pain just like it experienced going out of your body. One of the reasons why, you the individual has to get personally involved in the soul retrieval process is to be able to address your own health (with help or no help) for the life after healing. And it is for some of these reasons that the cure of the mind must simultaneously take place with the cure of the soul for the body to be healed as a result. Therefore, retrieve back your vital energies that are your soul's pure and true essence; divine and full of serenity and bliss.

These two books (Soul Pathway to Total Health and The Path to a Long and Healthy Life @ www.ahmedtatieta.com) might brighten your journey. You will get a lot of useful information and guidance in retrieving your soul's parts and for the after healing care. Verily, what is the use for you to gain this world if you are experiencing a soul loss? What are you really gaining in this life if you are showing signs of loss soul? Just like Jesus Christ asked.

Christ Said to His Disciples in the Gospel of Thomas

The disciples asked him: "Tell us how our end will be?" and Jesus replied "Have you discovered the beginning, so that you now seek the end? " For where the beginning is, there will the end be. Blessed is he who will take his place in the beginning; he will know the end and will not experience death". They asked him another question. "When will the kingdom come? And Jesus said "It will not come by waiting for it. It will not even be a matter of saying 'Here it is' or 'there it is'. Rather, the kingdom of the father is spread out upon the earth, and men do not see it." Jesus continued "If those who lead you say to you: 'look, the kingdom is in the sky!' then the birds of the sky will precede you. If they say to you: it is in the sea, the fishes will precede you." "Rather the kingdom is inside of you and outside of you. When you come to know yourselves, then you will be known, and you will realize that you are the children of the living Father. "But if you do not come to know yourselves, then you exist in poverty, and you are poverty."

And the disciples said to him: ‘Do you want us to fast and shall we pray? Shall we give alms? What diet should we observe? And Jesus said to them: “Do not tell lies, and do not do what you hate, for all things are plain in the sight of heaven; for nothing is hidden that will not be made manifest, which will not be revealed, and nothing covered will remain without being uncovered.”

“Whoever finds the interpretation of these sayings will not experience death.” And Jesus added: “Let him who seeks continue seeking until he finds, when he finds, he will become troubled. When he becomes troubled, he will be astonished, and he will rule over the All.”

Endocrine Glands and Their Hormones.

The endocrine gland is a part of the body that participates in producing hormones and then makes sure to also send the hormones throughout the body via the bloodstreams. There are few of them and their sum make the endocrine system in medical terminology. Each gland is in charge of a specific part of the body that it controls, by secreting or producing specific hormones to take care of a specific problem or need throughout the whole body. In another simple way is that one part of the body (the gland) tells another part of the body (the target cell) to do something important. The endocrine glands influence reproduction, metabolism, growth and many other functions.

In the end, the endocrine system regulates how much of each hormone is to be released based on the level of hormones already in the blood, or on levels of other substances in the blood such as calcium. A lot of things can affect the balancing of the hormones including stress, infection, changes in the body fluid system to the types of minerals in the blood. In my opinion, even some consequences of soul loss can affect your hormonal system as well. The glands are making sure to always have the right amount of hormones every second as too little or too much can harm the body.

They are: the Hypothalamus, the Pituitary gland, the Pineal gland, the Thyroid gland, the Parathyroid gland, the Adrenal glands, the Pancreas, the Ovaries (females only) and the Testes (males only).

The Hormones from each Gland and Their Effects.

- The Hypothalamus produces the hormones such as anti-diuretic (ADH), oxytocin and various hormones that stimulate the Pituitary gland. The Hypothalamus influences the nervous and hormonal system. It links the whole endocrine system to the nervous system. It is like the chief that checks the constant well-being of the body. The nerve cells in the Hypothalamus make chemicals that control the release of hormones secreted from the Pituitary gland. It gathers the necessary information from the brain and sends it to the Pituitary gland for execution. The pituitary gland in return makes and releases hormones based on the information received. The hypothalamus is located on the undersurface, at the base of the brain just above the pituitary gland and below the thalamus. The thalamus is a part of the brain that relays sensory information and motor signals that contributes to the overall decisions making. It is in charge of regulating our consciousness and alertness.

- The Pituitary gland in turn produces luteinizing hormone (LH) follicle-stimulating hormone (FSH), prolactin, growth hormone, thyroid stimulating hormone (TSH), oxytocin, anti-diuretic hormone (ADH), adrenocorticotrophic hormone (ACTH). The Pituitary gland influences the reproductive system, growth, childbirth, ovulation, sex hormones, breastfeeding, including hórmone regulation. Considered like the "master gland", it makes hormones that control many other endocrine glands. Your pituitary gland is as small as a pea and is located in a bony hollow, right behind the bridges of your nose at the base of your brain.
- The Pineal gland secretes melatonin that influences the sleep cycle at night and waking up in the mornings. It is also in charge of secreting the hormones called melanin necessary for your survival and protection from the ultra violet light from the sun. It is located near the center of the brain. The pineal gland is very small too and is shaped as a Pine Cone. It is deep in the brain at the very center and middle. Also known as the third eye connected to the spiritual body.
- The Thyroid gland secretes tri-iodothyronine (T3), thyroxin (T4), and calcitonin. The thyroid gland is in charge of the metabolism and the health of your bone, skin and hair. These hormones regulates weight, determines energy levels including the internal body

temperature. It also controls the rate at which cells burn fuels from food to make energy. The thyroid gland in the throat produces thyroid hormone in response to another hormone that is called thyroid stimulating hormone (TSH), which is secreted and ordered by the pituitary gland in the brain.

- The Parathyroid gland secretes parathyroid hormone that contributes to the regulation of calcium and vitamin D in the body. These four parathyroid glands are located next to and behind the two thyroid glands lobes in the neck.
- The Adrenal glands produce hormones such as adrenaline, noradrenaline, cortisol (helps respond to stress) and aldosterone. The adrenal glands influence and regulate the stress response and blood pressure including salt control within the body. It regulates also the immune system and sexual development and function. They are responsible for increasing the heart rate when the body is under stress. They are small glands located on top of each kidney.
- The Pancreas produces insulin, glucagon, somatostatin and others that influence the blood sugar in the blood. The pancreas regulates and controls the blood sugar level in the body (blood). It also secretes enzymes into the digestive tract to help the digestive system work properly. The insulin helps keep the body supplied with stores of energy in which the body uses when

exercising or any other physical activity. It also helps organs work as they should. The pancreas is in the digestive system. It is a long, flat gland right behind your stomach horizontally. It is buried deep in the belly.

- The Ovaries (females only) secrete estrogen, progesterone and others and influence female characteristics. Estrogen is responsible for the reproduction, menstruation and menopause. In the case there is an excess in the body, it could cause breast cancer, uterine cancer, depression, mood-swings; but when estrogen level is less in female body, it could lead to acne, skin lesions, thinning skin and hair loss. Progesterone helps the body maintain pregnancy and helps prepare for conception including the regulation of the menstrual cycle.
- The Testes (males only) secrete the major hormone called testosterone and influence male characteristics.

These endocrine glands are what make your endocrine system. They make hormones and release them into the bloodstream to induce a specific part of the body (cell, tissue, organ etc.) to respond. Those secreted hormones are very important to your body due to their participation to the major functions of the body such as growth, development, absorption of nutrient, maturity and metabolism. The chemical substances secreted will regulate the activity of cells or organs, the sexual development and function, the body growth and intellect.

To help keep your endocrine system healthy, you would need to get plenty of exercise, eat a healthy diet, add fruits and vegetables to your diet, drink a lot or enough water, meditate, sleep enough and worry less. Practice mindfulness and breathe control.

Chakras and Their Functions.

Chakra is the name given to the parts of the spiritual component belonging to the soul and our energetic field. It means wheels or disk when translated from the Sanskrit language. Chakras are spinning wheels of energy/light. They are responsible for keeping the energy inside our energetic system balanced. So, they take in energy from the universe, manage it, incorporate it, and emanate energy to keep us functioning at optimal levels healthy. They are the junction of the energy pathway facilitating the passage and flow of the energy.

Chakras are working in line just like the gland endocrines secrete and create hormones. Chakras are secreting energy when needed, reducing energy when necessary. In fact, there is a strong link between chakras and our various gland endocrines as each chakras is paired with an endocrine gland. It is not by chance that they are connected since chakras are in charge of making sure our gland endocrines are functioning properly and efficiently. The Chakras system that governs and controls our endocrine system is in charge of ordering or initiating the secretion of hormones, the distribution and absorption of energy throughout the body.

Unfortunately, the chakra channel can be blocked or simply imbalanced because of some of our bad habits and attitudes towards life. The truth is, that in our modern society, life is so stressful and the local food sources are flooded with genetically modified food next to no vitamins and minerals, that all combined with our lack of self-control end up sabotaging the energy connection and flow between chakras and glands, and between glands and organs. Our choice of diet, our environment, our actions and our state of mind together or separately contribute to disconnecting the link between chakras and glands, and glands to organs.

In sum, while the glands are responsible for releasing, regulating hormones after having produced the said hormones, the glands themselves are connected to a greater source of energy and order that are the chakras. Thereby making and emphasizing the importance of the chakras in our overall health. Chakras play a bigger role in our health that we should be conscious of not sabotaging them or letting them get blocked through our selfish and ignorant actions or behavior. It becomes imperative to learn of the things that could block the chakras and limit their optimal functions. The Chakras system involves your aura and the meridians that together make the energetic anatomy which I already covered in my first book "Soul Pathway to Total Health".

We have seven major chakras linked to our gland endocrines as follow:

- The Root chakra that governs the reproductive glands (testes, ovaries). They are in control of our sexual development and the secretions of sex hormones.
- The Sacral chakra, connected and linked to our adrenal glands. Together they regulates our immune system and metabolism.
- The Solar Plexus chakra is joining the Pancreas in also regulating our metabolism like described above.
- The Heart chakra is in connection with the thymus gland in charge of regulating our immune system and strength.
- The Throat chakra like the name suggests is linked to the thyroid gland and together regulate body temperature and also metabolism.
- The Third Eye chakra goes in bed with the Pituitary gland, producing hormones and governs the function of the previous Five Glands/Chakras (root, sacral, solar plexus, and heart and throat chakras) and sometimes even controlling the pineal gland. You should know that the pineal

gland is linked to the third eye chakra and to the crown chakra too.

- The Crown chakra, the seventh is obviously linked to the pineal gland and together regulate our biological cycles including our sleep and waking cycle and the secretion of melanin. Getting us ready to explore the unseen supernatural worlds. Now you know why when drawing the pictures of the saints, sages, prophets and healers, there is always a circle on top of their heads. It represents the crown, their achievements into the kingship or queen-ship.

It should be noted that the pituitary's main function is to regulate the body chemistry. It also regulates our emotions and intellect. In order to fulfill its mission, the pituitary gland works closely with the pineal gland as in partnership towards balancing our overall body needs. And to be able to open your third eye, the balancing of both pituitary and pineal glands have to be achieved as a condition.

List of Each Chakra and Organs, It Influences

- Root chakra: Testes, ovaries, kidneys and spine.
- Sacral chakra: Bladder, prostate, ovaries, kidneys, gall bladder, bowel, spleen.
- Solar plexus: Intestines, pancreas, liver, bladder, stomach, upper spine.
- Heart chakra: Heart and lungs.
- Throat chakra: Bronchial tubes, vocal cords, respiratory system, all areas of the mouth, including tongue and esophagus.
- Third eye chakra: Eyes, pituitary and pineal glands, brain, nervous system.
- Crown chakra: Spinal cord, and brain stem.
- Chakras and glands and organs work together and are inter-related/linked.

For example in a case where the Throat chakra is out of balance, the individual would experience some or all of these symptoms: Sore throat, neck pain, thyroid problems, sinus infection, joint dysfunction, shoulder pain, hearing impairment, earache and jaw pain or laryngitis.

When the Heart chakra is imbalanced, this individual will have high blood pressure and heart related diseases may arise. The inability to forgive others or to move past the past experiences causes the heart chakra to go out of balance. Slowly your heart hardens and exposes you to become insensitive to your own emotions and importantly to the emotions and feelings from others. At the end, love and compassion get out through the roof. Jealousy, hatred toward yourself and others, fear of betrayal and always holding grudges are signs of a blocked, imbalanced Heart chakra coupled with you feelings like a victim and losing sense of personal boundaries. Physically, the person will have a lower/ weak immune system, respiratory and breathing problems, poor blood and fluids circulation, colds, flus, infections and of course heart and lungs issues.

When it is the Root chakra that is blocked or imbalanced, the person present signs of fear, anxiety disorder, overthinking, depressed, feeling disconnected from the body, anger/rage and most importantly would lack sexual desire and in some cases the sexual parts may refused to perform efficiently or not at all. Traumas, eating disorder and fear usually block the root chakra and disconnect you from the grounding to earth. Physical symptoms are usually feeling drained, colon problems, bladder problem affecting the waste elimination, eating disorder, lower back problem, and left arm bothering you or lacks strength, cramps, pain and stiffness in your feet and leg, low sense of physical stability and feeling of not being grounded.

When your sacral chakra is blocked or underactive, you become confused, indecisive with a feeling of lacking control coupled with an inability to cope with the life continuous changing situations. It detaches you totally away from your emotions and those from your surroundings or love ones. Physically, you may experience chronic low back pain, ovarian cysts and other reproductive issues, impotency, bladder-kidneys issues, constipation, urinary tract infections, infertility and abnormal menstruation.

Emotional and behaviors dysfunction happen also when the Solar plexus chakra is blocked or partially blocked. It usually affects your confidence level, your trust level and your self-esteem. The person might present signs of insecurity and lacks the courage to take risk when it comes to business or other parts of life that involve decision making; due to lack of confidence and low self-esteem. Consequently, you will soon start having anger and self-control issues. Physical symptoms are: ulcers, weight problems, arthritis, diabetes, asthma and other respiratory issues, poor digestion, gas, nausea, liver/kidneys issues and hypoglycemia.

In a situation involving the Third eye chakra blockage or underactive, you will start having difficulty concentrating and focusing on one thing at the time. You will also lose the ability to process information and to have an intellectual conversation without getting lost in between conversations and ideas. Of course, all the ingredients are there to make someone lose their cool and patience under pressure specially when overwhelmed. You may end up vibrating low energetically and spiritually without being able to connect yourself to the spirits realm and higher consciousness, making you a good candidate to be fearful of the unknown and loss. Soon, you will be picking up low vibrating vibes from low vibrating energies and be drawn to negativity and chaos activities. The gate that should lead you to your inner realms and spaces of higher consciousness is therefore shut/partially and closed, disconnecting you from the spiritual and supernatural worlds and any possible spiritual growth becomes near impossible.

These are other signs that your third eye chakra is blocked: inability to plan or set a goal, narrow minded, poor vision/poor memory, lack of intuition/imagination, pessimist, negative and inability to foresee the future; migraine, seizures, sinusitis, sciatica, strokes and blindness in some extremes situations.

Finally, you will know that your Crown chakra is blocked or underactive, when you really start feeling lonely and disconnected from everyone and everything. You lose your sense of self and your sense of what you are doing or where you are going in life; just spiritually, emotionally disoriented. You lose your connection to the universal energy. This state of mind would increase your feeling of isolation or emotional distress. And the need to be in company increases mostly even it means being in bad company. Because of the strong desire to combat your loneliness, you might be ready to do anything to be accepted by others or more likely to do so. Some physical signs that your crown chakra is blocked are: neurological disorder, depression, nerve pain, Alzheimer's, insomnia, schizophrenia and delusional disorders, Thyroid and pineal gland disorders.

The Remaining Major Chakras after the Seventh

You have heard and read over and over that there was seven major chakras. In fact there are seven chakras that are directly linked to our gland endocrines to afford us an optimal health at all times. That's directly on those key parts that most energy workers or spiritual healers are focused to make you understand how your health mechanism were made of and how sophisticated your human machine was built. Now that you know about them, there are over a hundred chakras linked to your physical body in some small point spread out throughout your whole body with their specific locations. To be specific, there are 114 major chakras and 112 are distributed throughout the physical body and two outside of the body according to mystic knowledge. According to the mystery, 108 can be worked on and the remaining four would usually follow suit automatically as long as you get all the 108 chakras awakened. It is known and said that inside your third eye, there are 72 chakras alone just like there is an arc inside every person. And all the 72 chakras are as powerful like 40 legion of army. One legion is between

4000-10.000 soldiers making you with your third eye awakened as powerful as walking with more than 160.000 soldiers ready to fight for you when facing challenges and the difficulties in life. It is even mentioned in the Bible as an army of God's soldiers ready to fight. Technically, if your third eye chakras are not opened yet, you might be truly without protection and therefore vulnerable to the world evils around you. No wonder why the world's most powerful leaders are actively and low key wishing that you would not reach that level and become a walking weapon so to speak; incorruptible.

And it is taught at the mystery schools that there are 112 ways and methods to attain this blissful enlightenment and ultimate nature. That's why in most ancient cultures, 108 is a complete number for the universe and for humans. It is the ultimate full growth of human development just like reaching to the ceiling. In this book we are going to be interested in the remaining five main chakras summing them up to now twelve chakras (7+5) in total. But for your information, you can always awaken more and more of your chakras to perfection by awakening all 108th. Rest assured that only with 21 chakras open, you have reached the status of a full grown man/woman; 63, you become a sage/teacher or a master and beyond that you did really great and have joined the circle of the few, past and present.

It mostly relates the fact that we are interconnected and at the same time connected to the universe. And as an individual being, you are connected to the entire universe. Earth is the planet that ground us here and we are connected to the rest of the universe via a very thin like cable or wire or magnetic cord. It is known and accepted that, your cable linking you to earth stretches about three feet below your feet grounding you with mother earth to now up in the air miles and miles touching and going even beyond our earth atmospheric zone and deep into outer space. Proving here how the sky energy and earth energy can get mixed with our human body and energy once you are able to transcend high. Now here are the five chakras.

It is believed and taught in mystery schools that the eighth, ninth, eleventh and twelfth chakras are located above the head and the tenth one slightly under the ground. They go as follow: the 10th chakra is the energy linked with the earth connection; the 8th chakra is related to time transcendence and the ability to connect with the spirit. If your 8th chakra is in high vibration, it gives you a supernatural power to transcend time. The 9th chakra when achieved is considered the seat of the soul central for balance and the 11th one provides you with the strength and ability for your mind to control matter with a consciousness of mind over matter. Finally, once you awaken your 12th chakra, it open up the entire universe to you with an awareness of universal unity. Thereby, emphasizing the oneness of the universe within one consciousness. All chakras are not randomly put in your body and spiritual energy, they are there to accompany you in achieving a perfect/ total health and to help you reconnect with God consciousness in one universal unity. Just like the books and ancient records says, you become a god like.

What this means, is that in order for you to reconnect with the oneness in consciousness, you have to practice in awakening and getting back in touch with your chakras. Discipline is required and knowledge also, so that you will know how to awaken them by choosing a healthy and moderate life style. Put in the back of your head in remembrance that there is nothing else greater than the advancement of your soul to greater dimensions reconnecting you back to what was once your dwelling place; one consciousness, one God, one point of entry.

We routinely proclaim that we are a child of God and as a child of God, it is your duty to reconnect back with the universal unity. Knowledge will guide you throughout your way and wisdom will remind you of your progress and give you a hint the closer and once you get there.

Let me remind you of the significance of the number 108 that I mentioned above about the 108th chakras. The distance between the sun and the Earth is the Diameter of the Sun (864.000) times 108. And the distance between earth and the Moon is the Diameter of the Moon (2160) times 108. These numbers are not mere coincidence. It is a statement that Man/Woman are the ultimate cosmic measure and we are the measure of all things emphasizing that we were designed according to the cosmic measure. The bible confirmed that at revelation 21-17 (KJV) that "the measure of a man is the same measure as the angel."

How to Live Well and Prevent Diseases

Your body uses glucose as energy. Your brain needs more energy than the other parts of your body. The brain uses seventy percent of your stored energy. Seventy percent 70% of your energy will be channeled for the use of your brain functions and duties. You get your glucose from the food that you eat. Even though glucose is important for our survival, you do not need to have an excess of glucose in your body; then it will raise your blood glucose or blood sugar level accordingly. When your body is low on glucose; then it will be low blood sugar level. Either way, low glucose or high level of glucose in your blood causes diseases. You just need to balance your diet in order to keep your glucose level at normal. And usually, after a meal, it takes about one to two hours for your blood glucose to rise. Therefore, control how much you eat, consider what you eat and know what time is best to eat. The typical question continues to rest on you; as far as how big was your food portion that you consumed? What did you put in your food during the cooking process as far as ingredients and seasonings? And how was your food made? Fried, baked, or grilled, etc.?

At the end of the day, try adopting a heart-healthy eating plan for you and your family at a consistent basis especially if you are diabetic or pre-diabetic. Plant-based food like vegetables, fruits, whole grains should remain your basics everyday food to eat. Remember your body is made up with over seventy percent water, so you must eat food that tend to have enough water in them. That's why vegetables and fruits are always the first choices. Now that you know that your body is content with mostly food containing water, you can balance your food by adding a small portion of low-fat animal foods and low fat-dairy products while maintaining a good and healthy exercise plan. You can even plant your own vegetables and grains in your own garden to insure freshness and good quality of your food.

Medicinal Food Recipe for Diseases

GREEN ONIONS: it has two benefits. The benefit of onion and the one for the greens. There are a good and excellent source of vitamin K and vitamin C, and a good source of vitamin A too. Onions are rich in B vitamin as well which include folate (B9) and pyridoxine (B6) that play very essential roles in Metabolism, Red Blood cell production and Nerve Function.

Vitamin K is very important since it keeps your bones strong and helps your blood from clotting. Vitamin C helps protect your cells from damaging as it is full of antioxidant and regulates your immune health, collagen production and iron absorption. It helps DNA transmission and it is good for pregnant woman. It also helps cure minor headaches, heart disease and mouth sores.

We also have one of its relative, red onion that is low in calories as well and has zero cholesterol. It is loaded with Potassium that is necessary for our normal cellular function, fluid balance, nerve transmission, kidney function and muscle contraction. It is said that our body needs Potassium daily of at least 4700mg. It decreases

Cholesterol level, reduces high blood pressure and is anti-inflammatory which decreases heart diseases and elevated triglyceride level. Good for cancer and diabetes patient.

A STUDY OF 54 WOMEN WITH POLYCSTIC OVARIAN SYNDROME (PCOS) turn out that consuming large amount of raw red onions (40-50gper day if overweight, and 50-60g/day if obese for eight weeks reduced total and Bad LDL cholesterol (consult with your physician). Because red onions possess over 25 different varieties of flavonoid antioxidant. Red onion contains anthocyanin that greatly reduces the risk of heart disease when consumed.

It contains cancer fighting compounds and diabetes since it controls also the blood sugar level. It is anti-bacterial and boosts the digestive health as it is a good source of fiber and prebiotics that are helpful for the gut health. It speeds up the level of blood circulation within the body and it is suggested that Ancient Egyptians used to worship the Onion Bulb as the Symbol of the Universe.

Cucumber

Cucumber is high in nutrients, vitamins and minerals. Low in calories and contains a lot of antioxidants. It help Hydrate your body that could lead to weight lost. It also helps lower the Blood sugar level while promoting a regular healthy bowel movements since cucumber keeps your digestive system strong. By the same token, it keeps your gut healthy as it helps flush out bacteria as it is loaded with fibers while promoting good bacteria that strengthens your immune system. Most importantly, it possesses Vitamin K that helps in a case of blood clotting and promotes bones strength. Cucumber is good for Cancer, Cardiovascular health and diabetes. It helps fight against inflammations while promoting a healthy skin care. Cucumber has Vitamin C, Magnesium, Potassium and Manganese. It protects cells from decaying that can lead to chronic diseases. It lowers the blood pressure or hypertension thereby reducing the risk of a stroke and aneurysm.

Kale

Kale is one of the most important nutrient foods in the world. It is loaded with powerful antioxidants like Quercetin and Kaempferol. It helps lower Cholesterol level that reduces the risk of heart disease. It has a lot of Vitamin C, A, and K. Kale contains Vitamin B6, B1, B2, B3, Iron, Phosphorus, Manganese, Calcium, Copper, Potassium and Magnesium. Adding Kale in your diet will help you manage your blood pressure, boost your digestive health, protect you against cancer and type 2 diabetes. It will also provide you with your daily need with some of the most important vitamins and minerals. It also possesses antioxidants that help the body remove unwanted toxins resulted from either natural processes or environmental pressures. It attacks those free radical out of the body before they can damage the body cells.

Cilantro/ Coriander/ Seed

Cilantro is a good source of antioxidants. It contains vitamin C, vitamin A and vitamin K, E. When using cilantro in your food, it also provides you with a trace amounts of Folate, Potassium, Calcium, Iron, Magnesium, Choline, Beta-carotene, Beta-cryptoxanthin, Lutein and Zeaxanthin. Cilantro reduces the risk of heart disease, diabetes, obesity, cancer, and seizure severity according to various researchers. It also helps raise the body energy level and promotes healthy hair and skin. Cilantro has always been used as an alternative medicine supplement as it is anti-epileptic, anti-depressant, anti-convulsant and anti-inflammatory.

In addition, it rids your body of Heavy Metals, protects against oxidative stress, lowers anxiety and improves sleep as well as it lowers the sugar level in the blood. Cilantro consumption helps protect against cardiovascular disease and prevents the urinary tracts from getting infected. Good for the digestive system, cilantro protects against food poisoning and a real friend for ladies during their menstrual cycle as it supports healthy menstrual function. It is good for the brain as it prevents Neurological Inflammation and would also protect against Colon Cancer. Eat cilantro more often.

Mint

Mint is really good in nutrients and could be used to improve Irritable Bowel Syndrome thereby, by also relieving indigestion. It could improve Brain Function (brain power) as well as easing pain from breastfeeding. Mint possesses antioxidants properties. Its intake manages blood sugar levels and helps treat skin conditions. It also helps with breathing disorder and is very cooling. It treats common colds, headaches, oral care, aids in weight loss, nausea and asthma. Mint is an adaptogen since it relieves the mind from stress and depression and helps ease symptoms of morning sickness too. I discussed the adaptogens herbs in my second book called "The Path to a Long and Healthy Life" already, in case you need more information.

Radish

Radish is a power source of potassium, vitamin C and fiber. Radish detoxifies the stomach and the digestive system. It controls the blood pressure making it great for at risk patients for heart disease. It also cleanse the liver in the process. Radish has been used to treat Jaundice because it can get rid of excess Bilirubin. And by getting rid of that particular property, contributes to purifying your Blood. Bilirubin is a substance in the blood that also needs to get balanced so that the blood doesn't have an excess level that leads to unclean blood. Bilirubin comes from the breakdown of red blood cells and is excreted out by the liver. It checks someone suffering with Hypothyroidism too thanks to its sulphureted content.

In addition radish is a friend to our red blood cells as it protects them from getting damage thereby increasing our oxygen supply into our blood stream. It regulates the Bile production, safeguard your liver and gall bladder, as well as it helps in cases of water retention. And according to Ayurveda, radish is known to have a cooling effect on the blood.

Because of its high Vitamin C possession, it prevents against common flu and cold and at the same time helps boost the Immune System. Other diseases it would help cure are: Nausea, Obesity, Acidity, Gastric problems, Atherosclerosis, Gastric Ulcers, Boost our blood vessels; Good for the Skin, bile disorder, fever, sore throat, inflammation and Hydrate. It contains Zinc, Phosphorus, calcium, Copper, Iron, magnesium, potassium, folate, riboflavin, niacin, sodium, Vitamins A, E, C, B6, and K, high on antioxidant and vitamins and minerals. Most importantly, radish has a compound that transforms into Isothiocyanates which help purge the body of Cancer causing substances and greatly prevent tumor development.

The fiber in radish helps prevent constipation by moving waste around smoothly throughout the intestines. Fiber also manages your blood sugar levels and lowers your cholesterol level as well. Radish has anti-fungal properties that may help in a case of Vaginal Yeast infections, oral yeast infections (thrush) and invasive candidiasis. It is also anti-microbial that contributes in reducing the Zen effect on human when the corn and produce are contaminated.

Dates

Dates help maintain Bone mass, contain a brain booster, and help reduce blood pressure. It is a good source of antioxidant and has a low glycemic impact making it good for diabetes patients since it balances the blood sugar level. High in calories like other fruits such as raisins and figs. It has copper, magnesium, fiber, protein, potassium, carbs, iron and Vitamin B6. High in antioxidants and fiber. Induces regular stool frequency when just eaten a couple a day. It protects your body from free radicals and from unstable molecules. It reduces the risk of Alzheimer's, eyes disorders, heart attacks, risk of cancer. And is a natural sweetener.

Health Benefits of Burdock Roots (Gobo)

Burdock root, also known as Gobo in Chinese has been used as medicine and supplement over the past centuries. It helps treat cancer, diabetes, inflammation, and contains anti-aging properties. In some parts of the world, people with various cultures eat the root vegetable just like potatoes and yucca roots probably because the root has prebiotic qualities, encouraging good bacteria in your gut.

In fact, burdock helps lower blood sugar level, helps fight common cold, sore throats, viral and bacterial infections. Traditional healers around the world use burdock as a blood purifier since it also detoxifies the body of toxins as well. While acting as a diuretic, it also removes water from the body relieving people suffering from water retention. The fruits, the seeds, roots and leaves have also been used for the treatment of gout, rheumatism, stomach ailments; taken as decoctions or teas, it promotes urination, increase sweating and facilitate bowel movements as well. Among the many medicinal wonders, burdock roots may help with some skin problems such as acne, eczema, burns, boils, and minor skin irritation. It is rich in fiber and antioxidants making it a wise choice to add into your diet since it boost the immune system while regulating the cholesterol level and may increase your sexual desire. Consult your physician if you are already taking diuretics, diabetes medication, or blood thinners mostly concerning the taking of burdock's supplements. Note that burdock, artichokes, asparagus, or leeks are foods high in insulin.

Health Benefits of Ficus Seeds/ Figs

It has been used for a lot of diseases throughout the ages by traditional medicine men and women for ailment related to digestive, endocrine (diabetes), reproductive (menstrual pain) , and respiratory (liver diseases, asthma, and cough) systems. It is also used in gastrointestinal tract (ulcer and vomiting) and urinary tract infection.

It treats and helps cure anemia, cancer, diabetes, leprosy, liver diseases, paralysis, skin diseases, infectious diseases (scabies and gonorrhea) and ulcers. It strengthen the immune system, protects the cells, antioxidant, anti-inflammatory and fat-lowering.

One ounce of dried Figs has 3 grams of fiber. And we know that fiber may help alleviate constipation and keeping you feeling full and satisfied longer like you have eaten a lot of food. It helps lower cholesterol and controls blood sugar level. It contains a good amount of calcium that promotes healthy bones which can be good for osteoporosis as well. Figs have aphrodisiac properties good for erectile dysfunction and enhancing sexual desire.

Erectile Dysfunction equal three plants: Figs plus Earth smoke plus Chinese Cinnamon mixed together. You are now your own doctor at this point. Do your own research and make your own conclusions.

Health Benefits of Earth Smoke

It has been used in traditional medicine from the earliest times as a treatment for arthritis, liver disorders, and gallstones. Also as a Diuretic, a laxative, a tonic and for digestive problems. It treats Scabies and eczema (a lotion for clearing the skin was made by boiling the plant in milk). An infusion of the leaves clears the skin from unwanted freckles or banish the last of a summer tan. Earth smoke is used as a blood purifier, to help gout and yellow jaundice, "to open obstructions of liver and spleen, helps procure an abundance of urine, drives forth the plague and pestilence; to clarify the blood of saltish and choleric humours, the cause of leprosy, Scabs, Tetters (vesicular skin diseases), itching, scurvy; and eruptive breakings out and similar scorbutic affections of the skin.

"The distilled water "gargled often therewith," with a little water and honey of roses added, " helps heal sores of the mouth and throat, " while the dried herb in powder, including the seed, "taken for some time together' "effectual for morbidness and melancholia" (Le Strange 1977)

Wrote Culpeper (1922): "The juice dropped in some eyes, clears the sight and takes away redness and other defect in them...The juice of the fumitory and docks mingled with vinegar, and the places gently washed or wet therewith, cures all sort of scabs, pimples, blotches, wheals (welts) and pushes which rise on the face or hands, or any other parts of the body."

In 1750's John Hill (1820) wrote: "Some smoke the dried leaves in the manner of tobacco for disorders of the head with success: (Le Strange 1977)

The flowers and tops were also taken "macerated in wine" for "dyspepsia" with partial good effect. Still in the late 19th century, the fresh green leaves were prescribed because of their tonic principles. It is also aperient and diuretic.

Health Benefits of Cinnamon / Cannelle

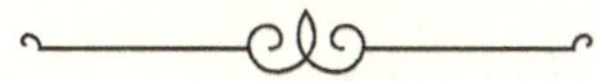

Cinnamon is high in substance that has a powerful medicinal properties. It is loaded with antioxidant and anti-inflammatory making it a good source that may cut the risk of heart diseases. It helps the body fight infections and repair damaged tissues as anti-inflammatory. As an antioxidant, it protects your body from oxidative damage caused by free radicals. Cinnamon is anti-diabetic as it is loaded with properties that lower the blood sugar levels; and can improve sensitivity to the hormone insulin. Even in cases where the patient is insulin resistant. Remember that Insulin is the hormone that regulates metabolism and energy use within the body; that transport blood sugar from your blood to your cells. Diabetes patients most likely become insulin resistant and cinnamon helps with that as it can even act on cells by mimicking insulin. 1 to 6g (0.5-2 teaspoons) of cinnamon shows that people with type 2 diabetes per day have shown a tremendous improvement. It has more anti-oxidant than even Garlic and Oregano. It reduces levels of total cholesterol, "bad" LDL cholesterol and triglycerides, and keeping the "good"

HDL cholesterol stable. 120 mg per day can have those effects as it would also reduce blood pressure. It has been shown to reduce the amount of glucose that goes into your blood stream after a meal thereby again helping to lower blood sugar.

In addition, cinnamon has an effect on the brain cells and functions. It has a healing properties that help with people that have neurodegenerative diseases such as Parkinson's disease and Alzheimer's. It will protect and fight against HIV virus and Cancer, Bacterial and Fungal infections.

There are two types of Cinnamon. Ceylon Cinnamon, also known as "true" cinnamon and is actually the best to use if in huge quantity daily. We have the Cassia cinnamon that is widely everywhere as a common variety just refer as "cinnamon." They both heal and protect.

Health Benefits of Bitter Kola

Bitter Kola contains vitamins A, C, E, B1, B3 and minerals such as calcium, potassium and iron. The mineral and phytochemical analysis shown the nutritional and medicinal benefits of the bitter kola. The consumption of the fruit can help ease cough, bacterial or viral infection and even anti-cancerous. It is good for food poisoning, diarrhea and upset stomach. Bitter kola reduces blood pressure making it suitable for treating diabetes. As an herbal medicine, bitter kola has been used around the world especially in Africa to treat various diseases like laryngitis, liver diseases, cough, hoarseness of voice and diabetes including all the diabetes associated complications. The tisane or fruit can be used to manage hyperlipidemia. In addition, bitter kola consumption is a common thing in Africa and is given to guess as welcoming them in big gatherings such as weddings, baptism, rituals, ceremonies and events celebrations. It helps and facilitate in good circulation, good digestion and boost the metabolism as it boost the body energy level. Studies have proven that certain compounds of bitter kola decreases the risk of prostate cancer and its phytoestrogens kills cancer cells and stops tumors from growing. Good for asthma, migraines, low testosterone, Graves' disease and Cushing syndrome.

Health Benefits of Watermelon (with Seed)

First of all, it is called water-melon because it somehow has a lot of water in it. Watermelon is hydrating. About 92% of it is nothing but water. Good to eat before sports, and good again to eat after sports. Due to its anti-inflammatory ingredients and potassium, it also helps your muscles fixing the wear and tears. In addition, it has enough magnesium and amino-acid L-citrulline that involve in healing specially after an exercise recovery. Less sugar with low fiber, it is a perfect snack and a very healthy one. It has antioxidant properties (lycopene) that contributes to helping fight cancer. Overall, watermelon is good for your heart as it promotes a healthier heart; lowers inflammation and oxidative stress; prevents muscular degeneration and helps relieve muscles soreness. It helps maintain a healthy eye and skin. Watermelon is high in vitamin C, A, B6, B1, and B5. Its seeds are rich in healthy fats and protein coupled with a descent amount of iron, magnesium, calcium and zinc.

Keep in mind that watermelon is still relatively safe for diabetic people when eaten in small quantity. Because it has a high glycemic index (73/100), it could lead to a quick rise in blood sugar level, but could be eaten like any other fruit with moderation as part of a balanced diet. Watermelon may help with some kidney disease and lungs health issues. It would help fight symptoms of common cold.

I had just eaten a good amount of watermelon and noticed that I was no longer feeling tired and sore; because my legs muscles were sore and as I was typing, that's when I stopped typing to actually notice that my little pain in my body was no longer there. I was then able to link it to my consumption of the watermelon minutes before I started writing this portion about watermelon.

Health Benefits of Sour Sop

Sour Sop, also known as graviola is a tree that produces a big juicy fruit that is loaded with a lot of vitamins and minerals.

The leaves can be used in treating diabetes, eczema and of course lower the blood pressure. It relieves mouth ulcers, get rid of lice; relieves inflammation, cough, fever, back pain, rheumatism, hypertension, and most importantly treats catarrh and helps cure Cancer. The fruit including the leaves treat liver, kidneys, respiratory, and urinary infections, and preserve the body gastrointestinal health. Good for people suffering from Anemia and those that have skin issues, as sour sop would take care of legs cramps while keeping your skin healthy. The consumption of the juice from the fruit, leaves, strengthen your immune system and prevents water retention, constipation, osteoporosis, migraine, and nerve damage. It promotes a good heart, healthy strong bones, boost cholesterol level and treats urethritis and hematuria.

In a nutshell, Sour Sop is high in antioxidant, helps kill cancer cells, fight bacteria, reduces inflammation and stabilizes the blood sugar level balancing the body blood pressure. It comes with vitamin C, A, potassium, magnesium, calcium, thiamine, fiber, carbs and a little bit of protein. It contains a trace or small amount of niacin, riboflavin, folate and iron. Sour Sop is aphrodisiac and diuretic and can be found at the nearest grocery store. It is proven that sour sop leaf can target 12 types of cancer including colon, breast, prostate, lung and pancreatic cancer. With no known side effect like losing weight, hair or nausea; it is said that it is 10.000 times powerful in slowing down the growth of cancer cells than chemo or Adriamycin therapy.

Health Benefits of Eggplant

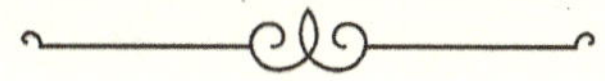

Helps with digestion. Improves heart health. Prevents certain cancer; and improves bones health. The consumption of eggplant may prevent anemia and increase your brain functions while promoting a balanced level of the blood sugar. It is high in antioxidant and may help with weight loss in certain people. It is actually proven that eggplant when served provides 5 percent of your daily requirements in fiber, copper, manganese, potassium, vitamin C, B-6 and thiamine.

The Importance of Breastfeeding and What Your Baby Misses When You Don't.

It is scientifically proven that when it comes to taking care of kids, the first very four years are crucial as it is a determining factor to the child life until old age. In kids first four years, if they are not well fed with the proper nutrients, it takes away close to 40% of their brain capabilities, thereby reducing the brain to only 60% capacity. Imagine then what happens to kids that their mothers refused to breastfeed or kids that are mal-nutritious?

I read somewhere that breastfeeding helps your baby remain healthy, smart and happy. It also provides all the proper and necessary nutrients in the proper proportion naturally. The baby can easily digest the breast milk as opposed to the cow milk/formula that is actually a foreign agent intruding in your baby's body and blood. Breastfeeding also protects your baby against allergies and obesity while strengthening the baby immune system as it provides the baby with antibodies that help fight viruses and bacteria as opposed to the formula (cow milk or processed milk) that doesn't provide antibody protection to the baby. Your own breast milk even prevents your baby from becoming diabetic later in his/her life. It is advised to breastfeed your child for at least a year to two years even. Unless you are disconnected from nature, or physically not healthy enough, the option of not breastfeeding your child should not even cross your mind. Who you thought your milk was for, if not for baby enjoyment and health? Can you really claim you love your baby and turn around to deny him/her what is the most crucial part of his/her wellbeing like breastfeeding? Please take note that there is no such substitution to breast milk and I question your sanity if you deny your kids yourself their birth given right to be breastfed, unless you are not suit for it. Don't just follow and take up bad habits from society. Protect your child while he/she is under your full autonomous control.

During the first days after birth, the breast produced by the baby's mom is high in protein, low in sugar and loaded with beneficial compounds. The milk at that stage contains every vitamin and minerals possible with the exception of vitamin D which can be given to the baby separately. For your information, studies have shown that babies that have not been breastfed are more likely in a higher percentage to get pneumonia, diarrhea and infections, and premature death.

Breastfeeding is also good for the mother as it helps her lose weight, helps the uterus contract back to its normal size, helps reduce depression and most importantly saves you time and money. Not forgetting that it is the duty of the mother to make sure the baby is healthily well taken care of with love and respect, thereby building and increasing the bond between mom and kid. At the end of the day you should note that when you breastfeed your baby, the baby grows up with confidence, with a high self-esteem, with a proud and trust. And that is love and priceless. If not, your kids will grow up disoriented, disconnected from themselves, psychologically unstable and less ambitious and proactive. Breastfeed your kids to protect them from the system and from them being contaminated at their early age with chemically engineered products. You want to produce a leader, start from the source. Do not let the evil eye feed your new born babies.

Your New Born Child is Who You Were During Pregnancy

What you feed the baby once out of your body is one thing, and what you were feeding yourself during pregnancy is another thing. Your baby is what you are eating during pregnancy. What your mom were eating while pregnant of you will determine your health, your temper, your tolerance level, your moods even your patience level. You would wish moms will be wise in choosing a good diet that promotes good health for themselves and their babies, but a lot of them are still out there eating junk food, processed food, salty snacks and sweet drinks. Causing their babies at a very early age to start having some emotional issues. A mom that continually eats those foods while pregnant sets her kid to be emotionally imbalanced and disturbed. Anxiety, wariness, moving too fast or too slow, getting easily irritated and impatient are linked to moms eating junk food while pregnant. Bad food shrinks the brain of the baby and increases inflammation in the brain. Too much sugar and too much fat cause cancer and diabetes and both are brain killers. And to you reading this book, know that emotionally and spiritually, whatever your mom were thinking and going through emotionally when pregnant with you, rubbed into you the infant as well. We are what we eat and what we eat is a representation of how we think since diet influences our thought and decision.

There are three different stages during the formation of a baby.

1. The pre-embryonic stage or the darkness of the anterior abdominal wall which covers the second and half week where the sperm and the egg are just getting in contact and mingling together in the process of a healthy slow ride to form a baby.
2. The embryonic stage or the darkness of the uterine wall which is now up to the end of the eighth week. This is where the sperm and the egg have given birth to an embryo that is of the size of a dot like a regular size of the average spider that you see in your household.
3. The fetal stage or the darkness of amniochorionic takes place from the eighth week till the baby is fully developed and sanely delivered. By the first trimester (week 13), if it is a girl, she will be having over 2 million ovaries eggs including the eggs from her grand-mother. During the first three months, the baby's brain, heart and other organs are formed. And by week 19 equaling to 133 days giving about 4 month during your pregnancy, the baby is now able to hear sounds from outside

the womb with the ability to even distinguish the different voices. At that stage, your baby could differentiate the male voices from the female voices, the tones with their softness or bitterness combined. That is to say that while carrying a baby in your stomach, you should avoid exposing the baby into toxic environment since voices carry energy as it enters the ears that could be healing or upsetting. By the way, if numbers matter to you, it takes 260 days for your new baby to be ready to visit the world. Your pregnancy is considered in full term if the baby is born between weeks 38 and 40.

In sum, when pregnant, the most important things to consider are your health and the health of the baby. It becomes the time to start eating healthy foods like fruits, vegetables, milk, fish, lean meat, whole grain braids and cereals. Also eat foods that have enough folic acid that is a B-vitamin to encourage a proper cell growth. It is also time to start exercising and drinking more water, while avoiding or limiting foods high in fat and sugar such us potato chips, cookies, candy, soda, processed food and fast foods. Of course it becomes obvious that some habits would have to be dropped in order to have a healthy pregnancy. Habits such as smoking cigarettes, drinking alcohol and taking drugs or any other substances that will hurt you and your baby resting inside your belly; are to be stopped immediately when pregnant.

You are Made from the Same Universal Fire Atoms

Our ancestors have let us a tremendous knowledge that is forever needed. They reminded us that we are made of atoms and that we should not worry and stress too much about life and death. Atoms are colorless, transparent, made up of infinite number of particles giving us a limitless boundary in the worlds of infinity. Our qualities are as equal to the same atoms that we are constituted of; Invisible, indestructible, uncreated, capable of self motion. We are simply divine and not replicable.

Even though, atoms differ in shapes, weights, orders, sizes, mobility, quantity and position, every atom belongs indefinitely to that which that is and that which that is not, the seen and the unseen, the physical and the spiritual. You as an individual can only be your own reality and through you every other reality is mirrored within the boundaries of that which that is not. You are shaped in different size than a mountain or a dog, but everything else around you carries the same original atom within and it is the combination of the atoms that contributed to the formation of this organic world you can see and the inorganic world also. The way the atoms are arranged makes them belong to the seen world or the unseen world seemingly compared to as the physical world or the spiritual world, life or death to be precise. Life atoms are arranged differently than death atoms. Life to death is only a matter of atoms rearrangement. When the atoms are arranged in certain way, life appears and when that arrangement is set in another way, then death will be the result. When death happens, the heavier atoms descent to the ground/earth and the soul atoms which are composed of fire, ascend to the heavens, the celestial worlds the soul came from. The mind also that is part of the soul is composed of fire atoms as well and together are made of the finest, smoothest, brilliant and most mobile atoms. Fire atoms are distributed throughout the whole universe in all animate object but in huge quantities in humans and of course stars, moons and suns. And after the death of the body, your personalities and senses disappear as well but the atoms live on forever; granting you an everlasting life or eternal life. That might be another reason why healers when it comes to treating a patient, they would also treat the subconscious mind of the soul prior; knowing that in order for the body to be healed, you must heal the soul first. Through rearranging or balancing the atoms and energies flow, with music, astrology, medicine and other essentials applicable health knowledge. It also helps explain why our ancestors told the whole world that everything in the universe is alive and possesses a particle of the Creation/Spirit including the trees, the oceans, earth, the birds, insects, hills, mountains, rocks, sand etc. Therefore every life and being are precious, deserving our respect and consideration.

One Consciousness

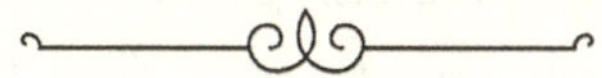

You are connected automatically to the global webs of the multi-universe. In a sense, it is just like saying that you are connected to God the supreme. It is not by choice or by a decree. Everyone regardless of their skin color or gender or height or weight is not separate from God. In fact, you cannot even separate yourself from God even if you wanted to. You have an authentic physical body, mind and soul which represent you and only you while you are still part of the kingdom of God. It may look like since we are billions and billions of people now on this planet that we are separate from the Universe, but we are seemingly globally separate from God and yet individually connected to God. God is the substance and you are the form. So there is only One Consciousness and so many individual consciousness from the reflection of the One Consciousness. You cannot exist without God, because you are the form not the substance.

Your individual consciousness includes your soul, your senses, your talking and thinking. Indeed your senses are parts of your soul including your thinking, walking, and talking. I guess that's why we lose mobility and consciousness after death. When you are dead, the dead body becomes lifeless, motionless, and can no longer talk either. Because the soul of the person has taken off with everything else including life itself. At the end, we are still individually connected to God the universe and yet separate from God but remaining within the One Consciousness scope. Our individual souls are connected to the Super-Soul of God the supreme. Each soul is just having its own experience and own growth. Therefore, you are never alone even when you think everyone-else has abandoned you. You are still linked to God and God can never depart from you because you are special to God; to the point that God will not move without you moving along.

What is Living a Conscious Life?

Living a conscious life is the same as you telling yourself that you will be living for you now; and not for nobody else or how someone else wishes to influence your life. Living conscious is taking control of your life. Deciding to start thinking on your own before taking any action without being influenced by a third party. Living a conscious life is breaking the chains of your conditioned minds and thoughts; by deciding to define your future or your life the way you picture it. It's choosing to do what is best for you positively instead of what society or even your family wants you to do. For example, understanding that it is the mother's duty and obligation to breastfeed her child for the long term health of her infant and for her, herself to avoid having to battle with breast cancer down the road; because breastfeeding is natural, humane and divine. Instead of following the new trend of disconnected mindsets of people thinking that breastfeeding your children nowadays even for a short time is an option and uncool.

When conscious, you think now before acting and each of your decisions are done after careful consideration and mindful thoughts about the advantages or disadvantages from your actions. You control your emotions by being patient and less angry because you understand that anger can damage your lung, kidneys even your heart; you become concerned about your own health and your own state of mind; not nobody else's. Instead of settling for a life that you might not like or did not work for, you take the initiative to do what you want to do in your life. You decide how you want to run your life instead of settling for the one that befalls on your laps. And that includes, unplugging yourself from the world wishes, desires and different views stopping you from opening your eye in order to reach the light.

Living conscious is waking up from your sleep with an attitude of taking and assuming responsibility of any of your actions. It's deciding to care for your life, either in health, finances, relationships and your environment. When you start assessing your health status and learn of the things you must do to maintain your mental, physical and spiritual optimal health is living a conscious life. Once you begin checking the health in your finances as far as starting to keep a close look at your spending versus how much you actually earn, and how much could you save when the unnecessary buys stop, is living a conscious life.

In a way, it is getting rid of, avoiding, reducing, cutting back and eliminating everything that does not benefit you no more with the right state of mind. Anything that does not serve you no more must be put behind and climbed over. Meanwhile working on promoting and practicing what benefits you and what serves you with a healthy conscious posture.

It is difficult to talk about living consciously without going spiritual. Meaning that it is the understanding that everything is connected and remains connected as a unit. In a sense you are never alone, because you now understand that for you to enjoy your apple, you know to appreciate the apple tree, the soil, the rain (air, water, sunlight, winds, oxygen, carbon dioxide, hydrogen, cloud etc.) and the gardener. Without the tender hands of the gardener or the care giver, you would not have an apple fruit. You become also consciously aware at the same time of the connection that even the bees, the insects, the bacteria from the soil played a huge role in the apple tree growth to produce fruits. You are also living a conscious life, because from the bite of the apple fruit, you know that there is a substance behind the fruit. You know now that it is not just an apple fruit; it is made of vitamins and minerals that will revitalize your body proving your connection to everything. Because what you need to survive, you have to get those substances from something else, from another being. That's living a conscious life, with in mind that nothing and no-one can live and sustain itself independently without the help from the rest of us and the universe many other living beings. Living a conscious life is being fully aware of the oneness of all things within one consciousness; knowing that God always provides and takes care of you at every step of your life and development.

You are also living a conscious life when you take notes of what types of vitamins and minerals your body needs to remain healthy. Knowing what you need is not enough. You have to make the effort to keep up with the necessary requirements for your body, like what to eat and what not to eat and how to get them. You cannot say that you ate enough vitamin C, B, yesterday and today you don't need them. Every day, your body has to get all the required vitamins and minerals coupled with enough sunlight and water. You cannot postpone, nor owe. Your body requires a certain number of nutrients, fluids to operate in a healthy manner. By the way, there are fat soluble vitamins and water soluble vitamins. Vitamin A,D,E,K are fat soluble and can be stored and absorbed by your body to be used as reserve days or even months later during runny days. Whereas, vitamin C, and all the B vitamins are water soluble, meaning that they do not stay long inside your body and are excreted out through urine, bowel at a regular basis. So, they must be replaced every day consistently. Every day, you should make sure to consume food, fruits, vegetables that possess Vitamin C and B because you have already probably pied out and pooped the ones you ate the day before.

Living a conscious life is drinking some hot black tea with ginger roots to energize your body when you start feeling low in energy. It is living in anticipation in preventing your health from deteriorating by taking preventive actions; such us exercising, eating more fruits, cooking more at home, eating more vegetable, drinking more water, meditating and sleeping enough hours. It also means, cutting off or reducing the alcohol consumptions, the drugs, the fast foods, the sodas, the juices, the meat and any conscious unhealthy life style. Living consciously has to do with everything you do every day. You are aware of your actions directed to yourself, and your actions directed to others. You are also aware that the plastic bottle/bag you threw on the street will make its way to the ocean and come back to you via a fish stomach in your dish to your stomach. You now know that you are an important piece or part of the universe and that you are responsible for anything from you that you add into yourself and into others. Therefore, live well and think before acting. Practice your breathing technics, meditate and retain that sound (chanting/toning/mantras), breath and meditation are the keys to awakening your inner serpentine energy and opening your pineal gland as well.

In conclusion, living a conscious life is the only way to live a responsible life. Instead of believing everything that you have been taught, you actually take steps to do your own research before getting into anything. Even when the majority of people embrace a certain belief, tradition and life style, you do not follow. Instead, not until you conduct your very own research to conclude and know why it is in fact good. Living conscious warns you to question everything. Even if your doctor tells you that fruits and more vegetables are good for you, you will also double check to know for yourself why fruits and vegetables are healthy food. From religion, traditions, to belief systems, you must do your own due diligence check with in mind that people always manipulate truth. You don't know until you have done your own research. If you don't read books and/or get informed, you will not succeed in life and there is no room for pretenders when it comes to living healthy and sane. Now you know better and must act better. Go ahead now with your fancy self and drink up some hot green tea with lime just because you can, and should make it a habit, daily preferably especially if sick; and if sick, add some raw garlic into your drink. In sum, living with the right attitude prepares the subconscious mind that is part of the soul to be healed first before the body could heal also.

Toning and Chanting Health Benefits

Vocal toning is the art of using your voice to bring harmony and balance to your cells and your energetic pathways. It is using your natural voice to express sounds that range from cries, grunts and groans in order to open the vowel sounds and humming on the full exhalation of the breath. It is a sound healing method that when sung, the chakras and our body centers respond positively too. Your voice is an instrument of healing. Chanting mantras and songs are also vocal with rhythm and toning is steady on one tone per exhale. Chanting is a repetition either silently or aloud of a song, prayer, words or sound. The primal syllable is Om (or Aum), and even Muslims, Monks, Buddha and Christians use this sound during their prayers. You can use a musical instrument such as trumpet, harp, flute, drums to rediscover the missing music in your life to encourage healing. Chanting can decrease stress, anxiety, and depression symptoms thereby increasing positive mood, relaxation and helps you become more focus on what is important. Since the sound comes from within, they are very effective in moving energy in the body. The benefits of toning and chanting are: -increases sensory perception and intuition – releases limiting beliefs – charges the brain and alters our brain state inducing alpha-theta states associated with healing – synchronizes heart-brain-body rhythms guaranteeing a state of centeredness – expands our life potential and creativity while helping us remember our original intention – rearrange and reprogram your DNA positively and most importantly opens the gateway for your soul freedom. Practice these sounds to strengthen your spirit and open ways for your spiritual awakening: Om Tare Tum Soha. And Yod Hey Vov (vouf) Hey to clear your creativity path and many others.

I will add to this paragraph as a bonus some frequencies as numbers given by the universe or imbedded within it that contribute to health, peace of mind, enlightenment and more. The idea is that the universe speaks in numbers, frequencies and energy that when known and taken advantage will improve humankind and all other Beings well-being. Those frequencies such as, 174 Hz (electromagnetic waves) may relieve pain and stress. Whereas 285 Hz heals tissues and organs; 396 Hz helps you liberate yourself from guilt and fear. 417 Hz facilitates and eases your path to accept changes in your life, while 528 Hz contributes to the positive transformation and the repairs of your DNA. The frequencies 639 Hz helps you reconnect with your love-ones, with nature and all other relationships and 741 Hz helps provide concrete solutions to the missing parts of your life or questions that you may have leading to the individual gaining full confidence of Self. 432 Hz releases emotional blockages and it is the best tune in music that promote healing. Studies have shown that listening to music at 432 Hz frequency for a period of twenty one day is beneficial to human health and mental stability.

111 Hz is considered the holy or divine frequency because it is the frequency number that helps and assists in cell rejuvenation and cell regeneration. This 111 frequency affects the brain by increasing the production of endorphins (chemical produced naturally by the nervous system to cope with pain or stress) which relieves pain and elevates mood, improves focus and memory. A study has shown that at exactly 111Hz, the brain may switch off its prefrontal cortex, deactivating the language center, and temporary switch from left to right-sided dominance that is responsible for higher intuition, creativity, holistic processing, and even inducing a state of meditation or what we commonly call a trance. Some Ancient temples and healing places were built to resonate the specific frequency 111Hz in order to induce health, wellness, happiness, self-awareness and the increase connection to our inner-self.

At the end, I want you also to retain the facts that everything moves, everything vibrates and nothing on this planets remains constant. We are frequencies, vibrations and energies. Even the solid rock, metal vibrate. Not forgetting any liquid or gas; nothing stays still, everything is in constant motion. So, human-being vibrates and everything else around humans also vibrates. What we have here is vibration upon vibration, vibrations colliding into others vibrations and so forth. Each one vibrating in its own frequency but affecting positively or negatively other beings with no capabilities to do otherwise as it is law that everything must vibrate continuously with no end. The point I want to make here is that vibration affects others and the environment and their environment.

The Frequencies of a Healthy Human Being

- The Thyroid and Parathyroid Glands: 62-68 MHz (Megahertz– an electro-magnetic wave frequency)
- The Thymus Glands: 65-68 MHz
- The Heart: 67-70 MHz
- The Lungs: 58-65 MHz
- The Liver: 55-60 MHz
- The Stomach: 58-65 MHz
- The Pancreas: 60-70 MHz
- The Descending colon: 58-63 MHz
- The Ascending Colon: 50-60 MHz

What you must retain in this paragraph is that even your different body organs have their own specific frequencies and vibrate as well. Overall, there is a frequency level for the whole human body not to drop below. That frequency number is 58 MHz and when that happens, the whole body health gets compromised. It leads also to a decrease in immune system strength, to weakness of the body and organs that eventually opens door for sickness. The normal and optimal frequency for a healthy human is 62-70 MHz and MHz means in our generation science megahertz that is known again for electromagnetic frequencies/waves or if you want the energies buried within the unseen universe.

When there are laps in frequencies within the body, you have to bring order within to the chaos within the frequencies as well. Various techniques can be used. We have modern medicine, herbs, sounds waives, gung, vibration therapy, and sound meditation etc. The higher your frequency, the greater your understanding and awareness of your environment; and the healthier you are in mind, in Spirit, in soul and in body.

Inspirational Thoughts for Healthy Self-Esteem

The world will not give you the validation you need in due time. It would not even accredit to you that is due and done by you if not because of some light rules.

When you wait for the validation from your friends and love ones before undertaking a journey, it is always a painful wait and most enduring because you may not get the expected validation from everyone or none at all. The lesson is in itself so that you would grow and learn that you just have to do what you have to do and not worry about what others think.

You might be highly respected in your field of study or your business line, or in your neighborhood, but the people that knew you before and have a certain relationship to you prior to your promotion may still want to treat you like shit. Don't bother to school them or induce them in dealing with you with high respect and consideration. Because those two events are purely separate; you that they knew to be and the now you that you have become. Do not waste time and energy because they might still doubt a good prescribed solution to a problem from you. Better yet let them double check every solution you rendered to them with someone-else expertise to turn around and confirm that you were right.

Do not look to others for validation, for your self-esteem can only be dealt within you. It is a you issue. It is your issue, not others people's. You are the one that is still second guessing and in need for validation. People that know themselves do no longer wait for anyone's approval or validation for self-fulfillment.

Now what would you expect anyway? The world never gives you what you want. Everything you have, you had to earn it, and so is your self-esteem and confidence. Nobody would hand it to you and rest assured that if you really wait for your friends' and family validations before being and doing who you are, you might second guess yourself for the rest of your life. Because you will not be granted that from the world.

Even the love of self has to practice. The value you place your self as a price if you were for sale. Some people sell themselves low, and some high and even higher than they actually cost. Everyone values himself/herself with different criteria; some based on intelligence, smartness, beauty, gender, and how superficially nice and sexy their body looks. Some others value their spirits, soul and energy that flows within them and others. Next to that you would also meet the ones that call themselves queens, kings, Divas, but their ways of life and actions do not match up with their own evaluation.

The question might remain. What if I just want to crust your self-esteem? What if I just want to discriminate against you? Why validate you and make you superior to me in achievement knowing that I could not measure up?

Well I will just have to keep pushing you down and low key rejecting and degrading you as long as I can so that me, my person could keep his own validation.

Have you ever tried to understand that you may not be the only one seeking validation to boost your self-esteem? Everyone does or has learned from it. The ones putting you down feel elevated when they are crunching you. It feeds their ego and make them feel good. So the next time you feel the need to wait for someone's approval before moving yourself to the next level, think again and keep on moving up because no sane validation could come from a world full of psychos and ego loving societies. Except from the few honest ones.

Knowledge and Wisdom Have No Cultural Belonging

Often time we get tempted to pick and choose the teachings of the various teachers and wise men based on their selective appurtenance to a culture, a race or geographical location. I have heard people saying that this is not my culture, and we were never brought up in that way of the life style of another region of the world. For example, when talking about meditation, a lot of people have a tendency to ascertain that it is only for the Buddhist, the monks or those seeking enlightenment; but meditation is a technique to release stress, to unite the person with the spirit and to facilitate the grounding of the person by balancing the different chakras and endocrine glands for a better health. Meditation stimulates your mind and helps balance your hormones, your blood pressure, your blood flow and makes ways for a better oxygenation of the whole organism. Meditation should be included in your life style. Not because you want to be enlightened, but simply because you need to stay healthy and sane. So it is not just a practice from India or China or Japan, it is for everyone universally. And all it might take could be five to more minutes of your time to breathe life back into your soul and body.

Another thing is the word chakras. When you start talking about chakra to someone that never heard of it, most of the time they only think of the Buddha which is normal. But in the back of their heads, some may speculate that this is a believe system that only applies to that particular region of the people that practice mindfulness. The fact is that chakra is not being taught in the conventional modern world and anything else besides the western mindset, for some people should be disregarded.

I'm here to tell you that knowledge and wisdom have no boundaries nor an ownership belonging to just certain parts of the world. And if you are serious in bettering yourself, do not limit your mind and consciousness to be selective on your journey to a total health connecting back to the primal source of Life. Every subject and discipline deserve the same attention and devotement from you.

The same goes with people that proclaim to be spiritual, and yet in their search of knowledge limit themselves to picking and choosing what being spiritual is supposed to be. "That is African or Indigenous tribal belief system". The truth is that without knowledge and without enough accumulated knowledge, it is hard for the mind to grow higher in consciousness with the possibility of accessing wisdom. Stop being prejudicial because without the knowledge of the different Laws and their applications daily to favor your life, it becomes very hard to awaken the Fire and Light within oneself. In your search of the truth, let the truth hit you and you will know that the truth always prevails. Your inner-self knows the truth when it encounters it. Yes, some practices will be foreign to you but that does not take away their legitimacy and pertinence concerning your life. The truth is not concerned about your religious affiliation nor your gender or status. The Law remains the Law and even planets and greater and lesser other beings respect and follow the Law. The All is mental. Meaning that the Universe is mental and with your mind only that you can win. The All is mind and we are swimming in it and yet the owner of the All mind is separate from Us and the Universe all inclusive. Know the Laws and you will be able to use the greater Laws against the lesser Laws to guarantee yourself a sane, healthy and prosperous life. Learn the forces of the natural life and universe and you will unlock the secrets in living healthy in communion with the Spirit. Those that seek will always find in due time. Those that knock will see their doors open in due time. Those that ask will also be answered in due time. Only when you yearn for the truth, you will find it; and light comes to those that thrive for it with no discrimination nor country of origin. And it is never late to seek knowledge regardless of how old or late you think you are.

I have met a lot of people that are so afraid of learning something new. They are quick to dismiss you by saying "this is not for me. *This one is African belief or Asian stuff. I was raised Christian or Muslim and I believe in my Lord only."* Fine, you believe in your lord but you don't know what your lord knew as far as knowledge and wisdom are concerned. How was he coping with stress? And what was the actual teaching that your lord was providing to his disciples? Can it be any other thing but teaching the Law? You know that there is nothing new under the Sun and the world is not merely 8000 years old; it is actually billions of years old (approximately 14 billion years or more) but the Law never changed.

To make it easy for you to understand, in no history has ever been a record of a man getting pregnant naturally and giving birth. Our needs for food, water and shelter remain the same either you were living 28 million years ago alongside the Guadalupe woman or 100.000 years ago alongside some of the Homo sapiens when they were migrating from Africa to populate Europe and Asia or today. Oxygen remains a necessity for life and the law for the rain to fall still abides by its own principles. Nothing is indeed new and the world has had thousands of thousands of teachers of the way to the Light, even millions. The principle of cause and effect still applies to our lives. The laws of gravity are still active including the laws of compensation and polarization, etc.

To sum it up my friend, the world never meets you half way. You have to make ways for your own salvation and you will not be able to reach your higher goals without knowledge, and knowledge of the Laws. In my first and second book, there are a lot of Laws included there also that you could make good use of. And of course, in continuing your journey in search of truth and the way, eventually you will find other Laws that could benefit us all further. Just imagine how many thousands or millions of civilizations might be existing in different planets alongside right now to our planet in this same universe that we are not even aware of?

Yes you belong to a religion already that you share the belief system. Does that stop you from acquiring more knowledge and wisdom for your own personal growth? I think not. When it comes to your health, every available knowledge must be considered. You are swallowing pills from modern medicine as I'm typing right now but you are reluctant to understand what other civilizations have brought to this world. Why do you think a wedding procedure is different from a funeral procedure? Because of the Law and the different circumstances surrounding both events. Either you want it or not, you will still be in contact with the electro-magnetism from the earth just like you cannot see the very oxygen you are breathing. An element that you cannot survive without but yet you don't even truly know what it is and how oxygen came about to be. By the way, the universe is not made of atoms like we have been taught in school. It is made of a dark energy that is larger than the universe itself. Dark energy and dark matter are holding the entire universe together. But atoms still exist though.

Now do you think you have an option to consider every other avenue when it comes to knowledge? No single book can ever hold all of the knowledge in the universe. Then that book will never be finished and published. No book is holy and conclusive. What about the giants that have lived on earth prior to us? Giants about 9 to 12 feet tall with a head more than twice our regular heads size. Did you know of their existence? Anyway, after all, seek the secrets because they are never hidden for the righteous ones. Seek the key to the time and space and you shall be free. Remember that time does not exist. Time does not move. It is you that is in movement. The All is absolute and cannot be contained or categorized, not alone given a name. The All cannot be decreased nor any possibility of adding anything else. It always remains and no other powers can restrict it. The truth is, no-one ever knows the All but the only thing we know is that it has no end. The All cannot be mixed with emotions nor feelings because the All is above any emotion and Feelings. It is above any Law, any gender and is One. The All is what you call God. Some call it Mysterious or Spirit; and there is no opposing force working against the All like the idea you have been trained to believe as Satan/the Devil opposing God. Yes, there are spirits and other entities fighting against each-others including human souls as well; but the All has nothing actually to do with it and does not partake in our humanly affairs since It already put in place a system of laws that work fine.

Mysteries sound like miracle just because you lack the knowledge to practice them or to know them. Knowing the Law is crucial because there is always a rise and a fall since everything including you have a tide. Thoth recommends that the only way is to neutralize the swing of the pendulum and in this case, mental transmutation is also required. Focus on the opposite feeling by cultivating the opposite to reverse your moods and emotions. Change your mental state. Use the higher laws against the lower laws. Cultivate and elevate your consciousness, that way you will be able to neutralize the forces from the lower consciousness. This way you may control the swinging of the pendulum by neutralization. The higher consciousness swing back carrying over the lower consciousness, yet you remain peaceful still and undisturbed. You have already read that the universe was mental. Make the universe a mere creation of the All in Its mind. For the All, the universe might appear like a dream but it is a reality to us since we are the All dream. Therefore do not ignore the natural laws, if not, they will work against you for sure. Understand the different movements of the laws to facilitate your own movements within, to fully enjoy your life peacefully with effortless endeavors. And you will not achieve that without using your mind full-power since the Universe itself is mental and governed by the All Mind. These are the teachings of our previous teachers of the law and the way that preceded us and one of them is known as Thoth the Great.

I'm from Africa and my country of origin was colonized by another country from Europe. So I grew up learning how to write and read in a foreign language. That language was the language spoken by the colonizer. I had no clue at that time since as a kid you really don't know much about history. I was just going to school and was excited to be learning the language then that was spoken officially by the elders that have been in school. I came to realize that the language was neither from my ancestors directly during that time frame, nor from any of the other sixty plus tribal groups of my country, even though all languages might have had the same origin. In high school and college, we were learning history and geography of the colonizer which really if you want my opinion was not important at that time. And when it comes to my country history and geography, it was like a flush and as soon as you blink your eyes the teacher was on another subject. Then I came to find out that the same colonizer had a lot to do with our country school system and curriculum.

Basically, a system that was designed to fail you from the get go. A system that aims to provide you with little knowledge and viable information of yourself. Remember that it is not in the best interest of the colonizer to wake you up in knowledge either spiritually or mentally. At best, the colonizer will always try to undermine and slow down any progress be it socially, economically and culturally. My point is that if you are in any country that makes you feel like you have been colonized even though free of movements, you should know that any school system has been designed to just teach you enough to be productive within that society. Most school systems are producing workers not thinkers, employees not employers. Because the day that you will start thinking for yourself, that's the day they will lose control over you and you are thereby now a danger of their society for refusing to continue being a sheep.

During my ten years of research, most and almost all of the knowledge and insight that I have acquired would not have been possible in an almost all conventional school. Because we are caught up in a virtual war of cultures, beliefs and traditions. We are caught up in between the west not wanting to accredit the east and the east reminding of the west how young and little in knowledge it has or is. We are caught up in between powerful people claiming supremacy of their cultures, religion and traditions over the rest of the world. So there is some hypocrisy in delivering you the knowledge from the beginning to start with. The east would not accept being dictated by the west, and the west would not teach the philosophy, spirituality, religion from the east. Meanwhile African spirituality and beliefs systems have been demonized by the west and by the Arabs; that it is evil just to further break the bond between Africans and their gods/God and to demoralize any African descent to even wanting to have anything to do with that kind of spirituality. Native Americans spirituality and tribal traditions have also been banned at some point in American occupation history. The slaves were also beaten and killed for practicing African spirituality or teaching their cultures to their offspring. In almost everywhere in the world, century after century natives have been beaten, forced to stop practicing their religious and spirituality system and powerlessly embrace Christianity and Islam and other religions as well in the past. Those that refused were persecuted and killed. The point I want you to understand is that religion has nothing to do with God. It is an institution run by men and women and that institution has to be maintained and must survive by all means necessary and adapt with time only when coerced. Ask Galileo what the church did to him when he dared to state that the Sun was the center of our universe and not earth; as for the church, it was taught to everyone that earth was the center of our universe. Either way, most institutions and religions have already been infiltrated by malicious men and women to cause chaos and division.

You must now realize that nobody out there got your back with some few exceptions. Somebody out there is doing the best he/she can to derail you from something that you don't even know yet. Remember that the motto of the world super powers is "divide and conquer". The less knowledge and the less awaken people are, the better and easier they can be controlled. And if they are going to infiltrate your religion and change the sacred texts in order to mislead the mass, they will do it. In fact they did it already. So it is now up to you to shake the bondage of darkness over yourself through being open minded and non-prejudicial in your search of truth and knowledge at least for your own health sake and for the health of your children.

You are What You Eat. What You Eat is How You Think

If you really think about it, this saying "you are what you eat" explains itself clearly. When you ingest food, your body will use that same food to produce enough energy for the whole body. The body will get all the required vitamins and minerals from whatever food you eat. If the food you eat provides enough to reproduce and reconstruct the body cells, hormones and neurotransmitters, you might be in a safe zone; but if the food does not have what is necessary for the body optimal function, you might have some health complication down the road, mood swings even anger issues.

Besides, food is not just some random food. Food is a collection of molecules, of energy, and spirit that once ingested, we become part of the food and the food becomes part of us. Each food has different vibrations, different energies and different messages it would send and spread throughout our body. There are foods that have high frequency and vibration, whereas some others are ranking among the lowest vibrations ever. For your information, food also possesses a spirit just like any other living substance in the universe. So, when you eat it, it will automatically become you. It will transfer into your body its best or its worse and that's what your body will have to deal with and make the best of. After a meal, you absorb the energy, the composition, even the spirits of the food into your body that would be expressed as a mirror through your physical, mental and spiritual bodies.

Food is not just to fill our stomach for fuel only. Food is medicine. Food is supposed to help us from getting sick through nourishment. Food should be a remedy instead of causing diseases. While food nourishes our body, it heals the body simultaneously; it prevents diseases from taking over our body by providing the necessary energy for our brain to secrete the proper hormones to keep the body's optimal health. By the way, fast foods and processed foods do not have enough fiber and some do not even have fiber at all; meanwhile the body needs up to 35g to 45g of fiber a day like our ancestors used to eat 50.000 years ago. The American Heart Association recommends 25 to 30g of fiber daily from food not supplement, but the average American consumes about 12 to 16g a day. That's a deficit of fiber every other day without adding the accumulated deficits of vitamins and minerals. Either way, processed foods and soda/soft-drinks beverages have way too much sugar, sodium, fructose and they can all be considered as poison and put your liver to work excessively since only the liver could metabolize fructose; and fructose is not glucose just like sugar can be classified alongside with ethanol, and you will agree with me that ethanol is clearly poison. For those that don't know what ethanol is, it is a dangerous flammable liquid chemical just like alcohol; but when you drink it alone, ethanol can cause coma and death. The same way, try to stay away from sugar consumption all together because that was not what your ancestors used to eat.

Food has the power to change your moods, your way of thinking including your way of reacting to the events in your life. Every vitamin and mineral the body needs to stay alive has to be collected and harvested through food. For example, blueberry could be a good snack loaded with vitamins and at the same time protects your body cells through kicking free radicals out of the body; good for the memory and lowers blood pressure and cholesterol level. Proper food helps your gut and your brain think normally with anticipation; since your gut ultimately also controls how you choose your diet, including your desires, will, deeds and wishes. Your endurance in life all comes down to food and how you spent your life feeding yourself and your love ones. Remember that every cell in your body thinks also.

Therefore a proper diet would increase your chances of fueling your body with what it needs without poisoning your own body. When making your choice of food, always remember that you will become that food as soon as you eat it. And that same food has the power to either heal or alter your cells, has the power to make you happy or unhappy, has the power to dictate your reaction and conditioned your decision making by interfering with your brain and hormones. If you want to think right, eat right.

I think, it is clear by now that the food we eat determine our moods, our tolerance and anger level. Studies have shown that some foods increase our anger level, intolerance level setting us up with a not compromising attitude or character. Versus, other types of foods that stimulate or increase our tolerance level, inducing happiness and setting us up to have a non-selfish behavior or self-hatred in making decision.

You know your brain needs Omega 3 fatty acid every day to properly function and to keep a good memory, so berries and strawberries would make you and your brain happy since omega 3 is linked to promoting positive mood and happiness. Studies have also shown that omega 6 (walnuts, safflower oil, tofu, hemp seed, peanut butter, eggs…) helps reduce anger. But most people have enough omega 6 and too much of it could raise your blood pressure, causes water retention and some heart function difficulties. Even though fast foods and junk foods are high in omega 6, they must still be avoided. The same studies stated that individuals that do not get the proper vitamins and minerals are also prone to become violent. There is a reason the body needs those vitamins and minerals;

and if not provided enough, it follows an emotional and psychological upset inside the body and outside of the body through you. The chain of command to stabilize and secrete the hormones and necessary fluids gets broken, altered or disconnected. Thereby changing your moods and thinking process. So my friend, to live a good life is to eat good healthy foods and to drink healthier beverages.

You Become What You Think

Successful people set themselves a goal that they will put efforts and time in working towards. Having a goal gives you the opportunity to spend time thinking about how to reach it. So you plan and learn how to achieve it through hard work. Having a goal keeps your mind focus and positive. Your mind works accordingly to how you are using it. The success that comes after the dream followed by your actions and dedication will yield money accordingly. Most people think that when you are rich that you are successful; but you can only be rich after you have been successful. When you think positively, your efforts will pay off in a positive way. Being successful is when you achieve your goals that you predetermined. When you think negative, most likely bad things will start happening in your life as a consequence of your thoughts patterns. Whatever sow in your mind is what you will reap. If you sow misery and poverty, so you shall reap misery and poverty. If you sow fear and self-hatred so it will be shown in your life.

If your mind is conditioned to think negatively every time, acknowledge honestly and make an intentional shift by thinking positively. Fear is one reason that keeps you from attempting to do better for your life. If you want to be successful, you must know what you want to do and apply those ideas with action. You must act to make your vision, your dream, your imagination a reality by making up plans on how progressively you will achieve your goal. If you don't set a goal in your life, you will not be successful. A man is what he thinks of himself. If it is positive, he will be positively guided as positive attracts positive. If it is negative, he will encounter obstacles upon difficulties in his life, because negative attracts also negative. You might need a leap of faith, but if you don't take initiative and actions to little by little go closer to realizing your goal, you know for sure that success will miss you. Therefore, you are what you think and how you think will impact your life positively or negatively. You want health, act healthy and learn how to be and remain healthy. There are always ways and laws to achieve your goals. Learn them and apply them with optimism.

Mucusless Diet Healing System (Dr. Sebi's Sample List)

Mucus-less diet has been proven to cure a lot diseases and possibly all kind of diseases. It consists in progressively changing your diet from mucus making foods to non-mucus making foods. According to prof. Arnold Ehert, "Every sick person has a more or less mucus-clogged system, such mucus being derived from undigested, un-eliminated, and unnatural food substances accumulated from childhood on."

It is understood that mucus clogs the intestines and colon and most of the time glues itself pile after pile to the point of obstructing normal conditions for a good digestion. Mucus also accumulates over time and adds up every time we continue consuming mucus causing foods thereby causing constipations, worms' friendly environment for/and diseases. In most-worse cases, the walls of the intestines and colon get lined up with a crust of hardened feces, a sign that the intense accumulation of mucus over time could render the intestines and colons inefficient. The system has been clogging up with mucus forming foods since childhood and that is why in order to remediate and get your health back, a mucus-less diet has to be considered.

Mucus-less diet consists of fresh, ripe fruit and starch-less vegetables. Fruits, green leaf and starch-less vegetables do not have nor contain the pasty, gluey mucus substances and are natural foods. When considering the approach of mucus-less diet healing system, the patient should be gradually changing his/her diet progressively by replacing mucus-forming foods with mucus-less foods followed by intermittent fasting. It is a system that cleanse and rid your body of the accumulated toxins and dirt build up in your body over time. And by gradually switching to fruits and green leaf and starch-less vegetables, you will be cleansing your intestines, your colon including your whole digestive system before mucus clogs all the system that usually is the cause of all sickness. You can practice it one, two days at a time while progressively adding more days to your mucus-less regimen. Some would prefer a one meal a day to start and the remaining of the hours from that day spend eating nothing but fruits and vegetables. Dr. Sebi recommends fruits with seed as you might have already noticed seedless fruits being sold at grocery stores. The reason in my opinion is because seedless fruits are genetically modified therefore no longer original and might potentially work in counter-clock of the immune system in the long run.

Here is a list of some of **mucus-forming foods** from **Dr. Sebi**: Fish, Butter, Cornmeal, Milks, Yogurt, Bread, Kefir, Buttermilk, Processed Meat, Fast Foods, Dried Convenience Food, Packaged food, Frozen Food, Alcoholic Beverages, Soft Drinks, Ice Cream, Vinegar, Coffee, Tea, Cocoa, Candies, Jellies, Baked goods, Marshmallow, Sauces, Chips, Plant Based Butter, plant Milk, Vegan Whipped Cream, vegan mayonnaise, all types oil, chili powder, curry powder, vanilla extract, pepper, black pepper corns, chili, avocados, corn, white potatoes, sweet potatoes, beans, rice, sugar, carrot and broccoli etc.

The **Mucus-Free Foods** from Dr. Sebi are: Arugula, Dandelion leaf, turnip, lettuce (all types except iceberg), cucumbers, Kale, Onions, Green Onions, sea vegetables, tomatoes, Endives, Dill, Zucchini, peppers (green, red, and yellow), Squash, Apples, Black Cherries, Cantaloupe, Grapes, mangoes, Black berries, banana, watermelon, sweet cherries, Strawberries, papaya, peaches, pears, Dates, Figs, Coconut water, fruit jellies (without sugar added), plums, prunes, raisins, raspberries, Sprout, Leafy Herbs, (parsley, Dill, basil, thyme etc.), Garbanzo beans, mushrooms, Nopales Cactus, Wakame, Dulse, Arame, Hijiki, Okra, Olives Tomatillos, Watercress, Purslane (Verdolaga), Izote Cactus Flower and Leaf, Curants, Limes, Tamarinds, prickly pears, Sour sops, Soft Jelly Coconuts, Oranges etc.

According to Dr. Sebi, you can consume in moderation those moderately mucus forming foods that are: Pasta, chick peas, Nuts, Seeds, approved flours, olive oil, avocado oil, avocados.

For your information neither of the list above is final and exhaustive. There are plenty of more mucus-forming foods and mucusless foods that are not in Dr. Sebi's lists; I just thought his sample lists might guide you in starting your journey in Mucusless Diet healing system for your personal well-being.

Dr. Sebi continued to bring us the laws of eating in rhythm that between 5am to 12 noon, it is best advice to eat fruits, herbs and water so that the body could easily flush and cleanse the toxins out. From 12 to 3pm, it is recommended to eat vegetables to replenish the cells and feed minerals, chlorophyll, melanin, and carbon to the body. Finally, between 3pm and 8pm, since it is evening time you can eat more solid foods but definitely no more eating after 8pm.

Random list of vegetables include, Garden Asparagus, Celery, Cabbage, Spinach, Cucumber, Sprouting Broccoli, Lettuce, Brussels sprout, Curly kale, Garlic, Turnip, Carrot, Okra, Cauliflower, Onion, Tomato, Parsnip, Potato, Collard, Pumpkin, Radish, Watercress, Jicama, Kohlrabi, Radicchio, Arugula, Artichoke, Endive, Avocados, Eggplant, Taro, Ginger, Sweet potato, Chard, Water chestnut, Black Mustard seed, Turnip greens,

Tomatillo, Chayote, Pea, Fennel, Bell pepper, Bok Choy, Mushroom, Leaf vegetables, Horseradish, Elephant Garlic, Lemongrass, Nymphaea nelumbo, Mung bean sprout, Galangal, Jerusalem artichoke, Wax gourd, Celtuce, Fiddlehead fern, Napa cabbage, Water spinach, Dandelion, Beetroot, Maize, Rutabaga, Celeriac, Yam, Parsley, Green bean, Bamboo shoot, Chives, Dill, Garden rhubarb, Snow pea, Snap pea, Bitter melon, Pineapple, Broccoflower, Daikon, Alfalfa, Cantaloupe, Romaine lettuce, Olive, Apple, Banana, Iceberg lettuce, Spaghetti squash, Zucchini, Leek, Pepper, shallot, Arrowroot, Amaranth Leaves, black eyed peas, black beans, Lotus root, Nopal, Salsify, etc.

The Importance of Breakfast

Breakfast is the important meal of the day. It is not just another meal like we might think. It is actually the meal. At morning, you just wake up from sleeping about 6 to 8 hours the previous night. While yoú were sleeping your body kept using and burning energy and in the morning, your body is ready to be fueled. And it is important that you fuel the body by eating breakfast. We might have built a bad habit of skipping breakfast but it is a healthy habit as every time you skip breakfast, you run the risk for your body to convert the amino-acids from your muscles as fuel. Rewire your brain and start eating breakfast again as it is the most important meal of the day. Regardless of your choice of diet either healthy or unhealthy, breakfast remains an important meal not to be skipped as it recharges your body with energy for you to start your day with vitality and strength.

The Teaching of Thoth aka Hermes the Great

"Wisdom is power and power is wisdom, one with each other. The inner power at the same time the inner fire is the most potent. It is an infinite fire burning day and night. The soul will become light and free itself from the lord of the night. Know that a man/woman is a Star bind to a body. And by seeking only the law, you will enlighten the great fire that is hidden within your heart. Know the Law because the planets obeys the Law. Understand that your body is nothing but a planet and your soul shall leave behind the darkness of the night. The way to achieving the light is to pursue wisdom. Only wisdom can get you pass the law. Wisdom expands your consciousness into the universe and will lead you to the pathway hidden to mankind. Get into the pyramid, retrieve the keys and follow the pathway to light keeping in mind that there is a war between darkness and light. And you the seeker of light, you will find it because light comes to him who strives for it. No matter your outcome, light always wins the battle. Therefore, always be a child of the light. The Sun is the symbol of the light at the end of the road. Knowledge will bring you wisdom and wisdom is power. Again know the Law and you shall be free because all exist because of the Law. Remember that time does not exist and you are formless. What is in the form is truly without form. It is only form in your eyes. Only the essence of the soul will remain at the end. Seek not the kingdom of darkness; the voice of the light is clear. Time does not exist. Shake up your bondage. Know that a man is nothing than what he thinks of himself. A child of light or a child of darkness? Light is order and darkness is disorder. Therefore, transmute yourself from darkness to light because darkness transmuted its light to darkness.

If you are a child of light, follow the path that leads to the Sun. You should aim at perfection because nothing counts but the progress of your soul and you should know that as a child of the light. At the end, all a man will be is because of his wisdom, and the results of his causes. Remember this; man has risen, man has also fallen. You are great but know there were greater than you. One God, One Truth, One Point of Freedom. Time and space are moving in circles, and on earth, men are on bondage between time and space. The pure must be in mind and in purpose. And they shall know the pure shall not be corrupted so that they may know that the truth shall prevail. By the way, death is not real".

Overcoming Your Fears and Doubts

Fear is merely defined as an unpleasant emotion that is caused by the belief that someone or something is likely to be dangerous. Fear is followed by the strong feeling or assumption that what is feared will cause pain or is an imminent threat. It is an anticipation of a foreseeable pain, an awareness of danger or failure. The individual fear is coming from impending danger, evil, without any possibility to determine if the threat is actually real or imagined or intuitively created by the past. An anxiety emotion over what actually your mind and gut are warning ahead to prevent harm.

While you have every right to be afraid for self-defense, when it comes to learning something new that would make a huge positive impact on your health, from you to me, why do you think your fears are coming from if you caught yourself resisting change?

Are you afraid that you might actually discover the truth? Are you afraid to know that in your entire life society has lied to you? Ask yourself this question. Why haven't you read the Bible, the Quran, the Bhagavad

Gita, the Torah and the many other religious books? Do you have an idea what are the principles behind the Mayans spirituality, the African spirituality, the Native Americans spirituality? Why are you not interested to know what your ancestors used to do? Why can't you try to understand the mindset behind a belief, a tradition or philosophy and ideals?

Sometimes we don't even know the origins and reasons we are afraid of certain things. One thing for sure, fear is related to the past. It is triggered emotion as if we already lived it and are now able to identify it. And sometimes we draw similarities and facts that actually might not happened the way our mind made us felt, the anxiety. You know that you can actually inherit your fears from your direct parents or grand-parents. Each one of us might have millions and millions of great-great grand-parents. So your fear might just be generated from everyone else in your family tree. That's how survival is instinctively passed down from parents to kids.

Descendant of enslaves might present different trauma, fears and tolerance compared to someone that have no direct link to terror and forced labor. If you already read my second book "the path to a long and healthy life" you will notice that I said that there was no race that have not been subjugated to slavery and forced labor. My point is that considering that we all have a link in some ways to real traumatization, real fear, near death fear, we should responsibly consider a life style that is knowledge friendly. We should overcome the fear of not wanting or caring to know and to learn some new skills/know how. A lot of enslave descendants and from colonization's might generate a tremendous fear of opening a simple book because their ancestors were brutalized whenever they tried to seek knowledge through reading. So it is ok that you don't feel the need to learn something new or accept any other truth besides the truth fed to you by your immediate parents or from your prominent society belief; but this is a matter of health and survival. Once you learn how to fix yourself, you will be leading the way for your own offspring's to be even healthier and resourceful with knowledge. Remember that fear can be passed down from mother-father to children.

We have biological fear, bodily fear, psychological fear, spiritual fear, past life fear, fear of uncertainty, fear of losing a job, fear of losing a loved one, fear of not being successful, fear of being rejected, fear of being deceived, fear of being killed, fear of being harassed, fear of love and the root of all of them is the past and the future. We have old age fear, fear of death, the fear of oversleeping, fear of running out of money, fear of making a mistake, etc.

The past is the observer of all and any of our fears. Because we are able to sense the fear from reaching in our past big luggage of fears from our life or previous life and past lives of our ancestors. Imagine how many grandfathers and grand-mothers you have had; probably millions of them and each single one of them is accordingly still in motion in you in some ways regardless of how far we go back in the past.

The past is somewhat the dwelling place of fear. The past has already lived that situation and scenario, triggering an emotional reaction. The past lived something similar to the event surrounding your fears. That is the reason why you should put an interest in taking care of your mind/conscious and health. And the only way is to be focused, balanced, open minded, tolerant to new knowledge and accept change because changing for the better is always good. Again, knowledge does not belong to just few people, knowledge is for everyone that wants to learn. And you must not think again that you don't deserve to know the truth. You are worthy of the truth and expand your curiosity while accepting what is and not what you wish it to be.

The master key in life is to always know the laws, and to use the higher laws against the lower laws in order to escape the laws through understanding the movements of the laws so that you can move around effortlessly, peacefully and calmly by using the full power of your mind since the universe is mental.

The World Calendars Systems in a Nutshell

These calendars are either simultaneously in use as you are reading, or been used but still relevant. They are the Egyptian Calendar, Sumerian calendar, Gregorian Calendar, the Ab Urbe Condita, the Assyrian Calendar, Balinese Saka Calendar, Bengali Calendar, the Berber calendar, Buddhist Calendar, Burmese Calendar, Byzantine calendar, Chinese calendar, Coptic calendar, Discordian calendar. The Ethiopian Calendar, Hebrew Calendar, Hindu Calendar, Holocene Calendar, the Iranian calendar, Islamic calendar, the Javanese calendar, Julian Calendar, Korean Calendar, the Minguo Calendar, Nanakshahi Calendar, Seleucid Era, Thai Solar calendar, Tibetan calendar, the Mayans calendars, the kemet's calendars and many more and forgotten calendars systems. As of 2021 CE, there are at least more than a dozen calendars that are being used throughout the world; or should I say that we are in the year 1442 when we go based on the Islamic calendar and 4718 in Chinese year? My point is to let you see that your knowledge and your perception of life or on any other thing could always be relative and short of the whole truth or facts required for you to fully make an informed decision or action without a careful due diligence.

Christ is Osiris and Osiris is Ausir

Ash Wednesday is said to be the birth of Christ during the ancient Romains era. It was also supposed to be the birth of Osiris under the ancient Greeks and ultimately the birth of Ausir to the ancient Egyptians or Kemet. Now, on Good Friday, it is actually the day Christ/Osiris/Ausir rose again from the dead. Coincidently, it is also the day the Orion belt is making its appearance over the Horizon and can be seen. Note here that the Orion belt is made of three bright stars and it is what is considered and also known as the three wise men visiting the baby Christ in the Bible and now showing up at the rebirth again and again. In the bible it is mentioned that those three wise came from the east and left by another route through the west. And that's exactly the trajectory of the Orion belt moving from the east to the west. Concerning Lent, it is the important and ultimate day for mankind spiritual awakening and spiritual awareness. It is a sort of a time out for the participants to understand and come to terms with their spiritual needs and divine awakening. For forty days and forty nights in the desert like what is told in association with Christ story, the recipients would observe forty days of Lent in isolation due to the nature of observance. Otherwise your surroundings people might think you have become a crazy man/woman suddenly. Lent is observed forty days before Easter and Good Friday is always on the Friday before Easter Sunday.

The Ankh and Its Meanings

The Ankh is the ancient Egyptian/Kemet cross that symbolizes Life, the after Life leading to Immortality. It expresses the balance between Male and female with their union assuring the continuity of Life. The symbol emphasizes the unity of the opposing forces pertaining that there exist a masculinity and femininity in all order of life. The Ankh is formed, beginning with a circle at the top symbolizing the infinity of the universe, the celestial worlds inclusive of the Spirit of Ra, the Sun god. It rests on Earth like the Sun on the Horizon, when the Sun setting or rising. And the cross representing the union between God and Humans and everything else's.

Also the Ankh is used as the key to the after-life when it is used to open the doors of the world of the dead and facilitating the penetration to the hidden meaning of eternity. At the end, the Ankh represents Life, Unity and Eternity; a symbol of transformation or transmutation.

Meditation Exercise Using the Ankh

Sit comfortably without distraction in some comfortable clothing without anything tight on your body. The aim is to not have anything pressuring the body including rings and tight bracelets. Take three deep breaths in and out, then allow your body to continue breathing normally on its own. Concentrate on your three deep breaths by focusing on the rise and descending of your chest. This concentration is to have your full attention to your present moment. And when you feel that you are in the now present, visualize white light around you first. Then visualize the picture of the Ankh in your mind in pure white light emanating positive vibrations of peace and health towards you. Receive the energy with humbleness and gratitude.

Do not exceed five minutes when practicing the meditation. Return to your breathing again and focus on your breath to close the session.

Preview of How Being Mindfull Looks Like

Prayer works all the time. Pray and never cease to pray. Forgive because forgiveness is the key to your health. Life is easy and hard when we know that fingers and toes come in different sizes and lengths. To keep your balance, you will have to find a way to forgive others and yourself. In doing that, it does not mean that you are weak, or too lenient; it simply means that you are ready to grow even bigger to a higher health. You may have forgiven, but don't be mistaking it as giving in, because you will learn from the effects that forgiving holds a key to your health.

People come and go. Every one of us has been given a chance to remediate our failings. You might worry, or overlook other people, simply because you might be in an advanced level, but the truth is that, if you are here on earth, it's because of a reason. A chance to grow again. A chance to learn more and to make a way for freedom of self and thereby, open a better way for others. Think about it. Everyone, regardless of their status, gender or sexual orientation, is already viewed as a role-model, or icon, for the younger generation, even for some old ones. It does not matter what is your level of influence. Someone, somewhere, will look at you, hoping and wishing to be like you. Unless you are a total loser, but considering that there might have been a time when you were shining, chances are, someone envied you in a positive way too.

You have probably heard this saying already. "By his stripes, we are healed." So I say unto you, by your stripes, they are healed. And by your stripes, they could be cursed also. My call to you; try your best to shield the youngest ones. Do not exposed them to bad influence because they will be the ones running, leading society and the world tomorrow.

Everyone has a job to do. Some like their jobs; others not so much. Try your best to find a job that you will find joy and pleasure doing it. Do not let your job and titles determine your views and thinking when it comes to fair decisions. Try to be as humane as possible. Do not hesitate to lend a hand to a fellow man/woman when he or she seeks your help. Whenever you can, try to intercede and help. Because that's the way the universe works. You could have been one of the last that have made a difference to others' lives.

Of course, people burn their own bridges but remind them of their shortcomings. If you can, put a smile on someone else's face, as that reward I can guarantee you, if done in good faith, will resonate on heaven's gates. Because that's how and why this universe is intended to be lived.

Remember; you have made your own mistakes along the way, and you will wish someone else will overlook those mistakes and still give you a smile, when needed. This life, when really understood fully, is nothing but a laughter. Because it's always a circle and its opposite; things and everything we do that need to be readdressed will always land in our laps for adjustment. This is the chance we have been given to always redeem ourselves and grow higher in the next course of the circle. Remember that even those that have had a total memory loss will always get flashbacks. Some will even still remember, in spite of the memory loss, things that have marked them, or what they wish to see happen in their favor, or others. I prefer memory disconnection from the cognitive mind. Whatever was stored is still there but displaced, or it might just need a new fuse to reconnect the system back together.

Do not expect that people will live up to their words, or extend to you a favor, even when due, and you know that that's the least they could have done. Not everyone will give you the respect when needed, nor will even acknowledge your existence. Just dismiss them and move along with your life, serving your purpose with a smile and no regrets of any good deeds you have ever done to them and for them. Know that when it's cold, everybody is looking for a place that is warm. And when it is warm in your place, and the ideal for the season is to get some air and freshness, the same people will vacate and go where there is air to breathe. We are a survival species and do not most of the time stay loyal or faithful until all our needs and expectations are met. Once you understand the logic of human survival mechanisms, then you will be free from judgments.

Also remember that each one teach one. What you know that would make it easy for the next fellow, do not hesitate to teach and share your expertise. Because without teachers, I will not be even able to convey this message to you. Because someone had to teach me how to read; how to write; and how to think. Teachers are guided and bearers of light to the least and to the extensive courses; because there are always steps to understand prior to the next lessons.

Always respect your teachers. Give them the chance to coach and teach you. Listen and always ask questions; that's the only way to fully understand and comprehend a subject. The future is nothing more promising than with plenty of teachers. So take heed and pride in teaching as nobody has ever made it too far without one.

Overall, there is no veil, nor a shade, over a star. Show me a man or a woman that has never been criticized. Why should we then vex ourselves at things that do not even care about themselves? The truth remains; one man is born, another is born again. And one man is dead and another is also dead. Look around at the courses of the stars like you were going along with them, by considering the changes of the elements into each other and into one another, without worrying if they would change your fate. That way, you might keep a peace of mind and control your life better.

With enough knowledge, you will come to understand the meaning of their movements and their implications to your life, your environment and yours. And with enough wisdom, you might be able to interpret and anticipate their movements.

Taking Care of Your Body While Getting Old

The body is a machine that operates based on a strict certain instructions. It's a machine that needs constant care, and must not be starved or thirst. It is no news to you that you have to take care of your body daily to remain alive and healthy. Research has shown that even though our health might be determined and contingent of our genes, our lifestyle actually plays a huge role in keeping up with our health. It has stated that about 30% percent of physical aging have to be blamed on gene only, but the rest has to do with the way you eat, the health risks you take, how active you are, how often you get checked by a physician or a spiritual doctor, and how often you detox your body. Everything is concerned about health; and the secret is that you have to remain physically and mentally active, and undertake preventive measures to avoid major diseases.

In addition, you must stay socially engaged by visiting and communicating with your loved ones and friends, and keep always an optimistic attitude. Eating few walnuts every day will reduce your risk of heart attacks by 40%

percent. While keeping up with your exercise routine, you must know that only exercise makes you stronger as time goes by. Drinking green tea is beneficial while aging because green tea has a high level of antioxidant (EGCG) believed by scientists to be most potent anticancer compound. Eat at least five fruits or five types of fruits every day. Eat fruits and vegetables like your life depends on it, because it is.

Truthfully, your heart health, your digestive strength, weight, blood pressure, cancer protection, blood sugar level, cholesterol level, all depend on you continuously eating fruits and vegetables daily. It is so advised, because fruits and vegetables are rich in fiber, potassium, antioxidants and folic acid; good source of magnesium, iron, vitamins mostly C, beta-carotene, folate. And they are delicious, tasty with little or no fat, calories and sodium. Studies have proven that man over 40 years of age that ate or have 3 or more serving a week of the cruciferous vegetables might have 41% percent lower risk of prostate cancer compared to those other man that absolutely don't eat vegetables or consume a little. The cruciferous vegetables are Broccoli, Cabbage, Kale, Brussels sprouts, Bok Choy and Cauliflower. It is important to note that fruits and vegetables are pretty much your only and unique way to get some powerful phytochemicals that shield and protect you from getting sick, thereby keeping you away from diseases and the hospital. Meanwhile, never stop exercising.

Nature Mysteries

Every year around June to August, there is a wave of winds in the Saharan desert crossing the Atlantic Ocean heading towards the Caribbean and the America's. These tall and heavy dust commute as long as over 8000 km reaching the United States, the Amazon forest, Cuba etc. The dust compact will be as high as 3 to 6 km tall.

This phenomena is not random. The particles of heavy dust is part of the ecosystem as the dust will provide nutrients for marine plants. Minerals from the dust will fall into the Ocean that will cause blooms of phytoplankton to form at the ocean's surface, which in turn provides food that other marine life could not survive without. Surprisingly, the same dust on its journey also feeds the Amazon. It constantly provides nutrients to the rainforest soils, otherwise at some point the rainforest will drained out of nutrients due to the constant rain falls. The same dusty air layers are known to suppress the development of hurricanes and storms in the Atlantic. For a storm to form, it needs the warn ocean water and warm humid air. Since the air from the Saharan desert is dusty, once it collides with the dusty and dry layers of air, any storm slows down and stop growing, preventing then hurricanes and big storms to form. Now you might understand when the wise people usually say that the way the air is flowing in any parts of the globe will produce a chain of reactions in the other parts of the globe no matter how insignificant we might think the force of the flow was primarily. Everything is indeed connected and does not contradicts the laws of the universe.

Another intriguing phenomena is the fact that the Pacific Ocean water and the Atlantic Ocean do not mix. Even though, they cross path and seemingly touches each-others at their meeting points, each water waves back to its parent each time at no fail and continue the back and forth waving day and night without mixing each other. It seems like there is an invisible barrier or border, but the two Oceans possess different kind of waters making their mixing quasi-impossible even though they merge and meet at the dividing line. That is the way nature intended it to be and each time the laws of the universe are again respected and fully complied to.

The Eye is the Light and the Lamp of the Body

If you don't have an eye, then there will be no way for your body to be full or filled with light. The eye is the lamp of the body. Without the eye, your light will not be lighten. If you pay attention, you will notice that it is said the eye, not the eyes. You only have one eye to see reel. And you only was given one eye only. Well, some might say three spiritual eyes since it usually starts by your soul being able to open his/her first two eyes prior to the third. Now if your eye is not healthy, your body will not be full of light. The eye has to be healthy in order for the light to shine over your body. If your eye is bad, you are blind and might be full of darkness. It is a condition and law that do not care about your feelings or what you feel or believe in. It is a law and the only way for the light within you to shine over your body, you must have a healthy eye. Once your eye is open and fully healthy, only then you will have access to the unseen, the worlds of the supernatural. Without the eye, you will remain in the darkness and your body will be cover with darkness since there is no way for the light to come through your body. The eye is the access zone where the light shines through filling your whole body with light. Yes the light everyone has been talking about being the light of the world.

If your eye is healthy, then you surely know what I'm talking about. If your eye is bad, work on getting your eye healthy first and you will also know what I was talking about. Remember the saying of the ancestors that you must first take off the plank in your own eye and now if you cannot do it yourself, at least don't resist when someone else is taking it off for you. This is what the Bible says regarding the third eye importance: Genesis 32:30 "Jacob called the name of the place Penial, for I have seen God face to face". Matthew 6:22 "the eye is the lamp of the body. So if your eye is healthy, your whole body will be full of light." And Jesus Christ to conclude that the Kingdom of God is in the midst"; in the middle which is the third eye.

The Secret Weapon from Your Ancestors

We know that you are lost. We also know that you have experienced or experiencing a soul loss. You have lost hope because you have never gotten an answer to your many questions. You want to know who you are and how in the heck you are where you are. It is not quite simple to not know about your History, your language, your culture and other traditions. Yes we know that you feel sometimes empty and robbed to the fact that no-one else around you remembers nothing. The books you read could not fulfill your answers, so you were never satisfied because there is always a lot to learn, a lot to find out and yet full of contradictions. At the end, some of you ended up hating themselves, hating their offspring, and the people around them without any particular reasons. Yes you have heard about your ancestors' great past and achievements and yet it didn't move you because you think that you are disconnected from your ancestors.

I got news for you today my brother. I got something for you too my sister. Look at the tip of your noise and you will see your ancestor's blood and physical characteristics flowing in your veins. Check the shape of your scalp and crane and you will find your ancestors in you. Your ancestors never went anywhere. They are still within you in your ears, eyes, butts, knee cup, chest, your voice etc. And you yourself will become one through your children offspring. Everything about you represents how and who your ancestors were. The next time you feel alone and looking out for your ancestors or some guidance, remember to check your smile and the way you walk; because your great grand-ma had the same laugh and have that nice looking walk of yours with a swag.

You are the extension from your ancestors bloodlines combined. Every-one of us has millions of millions of ancestors that are still linked and connected to us regardless of what society today tells you. The average span between generations is about 20, 25 to 30 years. If you go 400 years in the past alone, you have 20 generations combined. And 20 generations give you about a million ancestors. The further way back you look up, your ancestors numbers increase exponentially. 800 years back make forty generations with as many as one trillion ancestors of yours checking and rooting for you and yours. You will be linked to your kids as well even after death; because truly after death, you will just be moved to somewhat across the street separated by a thin spiritual or supernatural wall to continue living. Even for the souls that choose to remain on earth realm or for some reasons cannot cross over yet. The eye shall prove it to you.

Picture this, every tree produces its own kind. Everything in the fruit is in the tree and everything in the seed is in the tree as well. A lime tree would produce a lime fruit and the same goes with the papaya or oranges. Your grand-parents are the trees, your actual parents are the fruits and you are the seeds.

Besides, you have inherited who you are from your parents through your grand-parents; and your grand-parents inherited who they were from their respective parents which are your great grand-parents. The list continues down all the way to 100000 years ago, 2000000 years ago and so forth. Imagine how much strength and solid background you are wearing within your skin and soul? Think about it the next time someone tells you that you have no-one in your life. Just you alone, millions of your ancestors are living within you, expressing themselves within you through genes, karma, intelligence, strength, courage, insights, fear, endurance and kindness etc. Your ancestors are your guide in a way since they have accumulated experiences and know how's. And by the way, you can reach out to them just by thinking about them. The connection line is never so- broken; it only gets weakened as time goes by and when one forgets about his/her ancestors. Unhook yourself from the matrix of the world many events that have surrounded your life, blinded your eye and you will really see clearly and understand life better. You are not alone and were never alone. There is no law forbidding you from asking your ancestors to intercede on your behalf; and don't you let anyone tell you otherwise. Just be careful not to consult an ancestor that was living a foolish life in his/her original lives. In everything, there are good and bad; you pick.

I gave you this Knowledge for you to understand that there is no chain whatsoever that can hold you from achieving your goals. There is no such boundary that you will not be able to cross. You are the ambassador of your ancestors on earth and they are your ambassadors as well in the supernatural world. Each one represents the other and maintains the link for continuity as the universe never disconnects neither from nothing else and nobody. It is not about beliefs systems. It is a fact and connecting back to your ancestors might look optional but in truth, you are already doing it anyway. When you are desperate, hopeless and crying out or praying, they hear you and send you positive vibes and connecting links to intervene and help you without you even knowing it. Even religious people do the same when they ask the dead called saints to intervene in their worldly affairs. Would you walk away from your kids and grand-kids without helping them when you become an ancestor? I bet not.

Now that you know the truth, know thyself now by building your own individuality so that your ancestors might not be able to fully live through you, by making you live their lives instead of you living and tracing your own destiny. Remember that you might have inherited a whole bunch of positivity and negativity from them depending on the impulse of your family lineage energy and destiny. Helping you when you need their assistance is one thing, and them living through you and shaping your thoughts, wishes, desires are another. All it takes is you wanting to turn on your light within in order to know thyself and with enough knowledge and determination, your soul would surely join the table of the octave's festivals; when your seventh Soul with their culmination in the eighth one concretize, giving you the eternal fatherhood or motherhood representation. The eighth one (soul) as manifestor of the seven was also called Atum-Ra, Atma, Christ, Ptah, Buddhi, Krishna Agni, Buddha, Assur, Totem, Horus, Elijah, Osiris, Jehovah, Pharaoh, Vishnu, Caesar, Ra, Repa, Har-Khuti, Las-aru, Lazarus and Lord of lights etc. Once you reach the eternal maturity, then your soul will enter the status of the one living god.

We don't call on our ancestors because we are worshiping them, we call on them because we recognize them, because we recognize the umbilical cord. Don't let History from the past shake you up any longer. Get grounded, connect to the ground, drink from the vine tree and produce authentic fruits that will save your next generations. In a way, become your own savior instead of looking for one.

In order for you to move forward, you must accept this truth and recognize your ancestors to be able to fix your present and open new horizons for the new generation from you forth. If your forefathers did something wrong in the past that needs fixing, only you are in the position to do it by redeeming all your lineage past present and future. Remember when Daniel in the Bible was negotiating with God in the past; for God to forgive his ancestors for whatever wrong they did in the past. If you have done so and got your ancestors forgiven as the same Bible tells you that you have been forgiven. Therefore stop locking yourself in the past and live in the present as even what is written in the Bible for example concerning you resides in the past. You are no longer born in sin, as your forefathers have already been forgiven. God resides in the woman as well as in the man; therefore, take care of your business and help one another. You are a full half if I can say it this way and know that there is no other better half to look for in order to be full. Fix yourself first. Your first Estate is your mind.

Did You Think Life was Fair?

You might have at some point come to realize that life was supposed to be fair. To the citizen lambda, life is fair and always comes to find out that life is not fair. In our dreams we might picture it like how come life surprises us to make it clear that it isn't fair in real life. With all the injustices going on the real life, one should soon realize that life in question was not supposed to be fair. You put two single people in a room to soon realize that they will have similarities and opposing ideas and opinions; that could always lead to miscommunication. It might be a bummer but the sobering fact is that life isn't fair is an absolute truth in perception.

In the sight of our five senses, life isn't perfect but on the other hand, life is fair, real and just. All the possibilities of events that mankind can do, make life at some point becomes unfair. It is not life's responsibility to make the world just and fair. It is our own challenges that lead us to think that life is unjust and unfair. Who even said that life should have been fair?

Every place you dwell on this planet earth is merely only top soil of other previous living beings without any exclusion of all the species that have walk, swim, fly, cramped, float, road, etc.

Don't feel sorry for feeling that the world is fair. Instead, realize that maybe life was not even intended to be fair. Rid yourself of the idea that life is fair and stop feeling sorry for yourself and for others.

Remember that each ones have their own strength, their own challenges, and their own perception of what they chose to believe and entertain. We each chose what to tolerate, to act on and/or when to opinionate or remain silent. Give it a thought to our own struggle; your addictions, your wishes and desires, you would realize that alone might suggest to you that life was not meant to be fair. People get cheated at, lied to, abused, and at the same time the same very people get love and respect for others in different circumstances. Life encourages us to do our very best day by day concentrating to becoming a better person here and there, until we achieve the ultimate level of comprehension of how to live and be happy with ourselves for us, not for no-one else's. You have the capabilities and the power to improve yourself and the world. And you must act on improving yourself and by stopping to feel pity instead of having loving compassion towards yourself and for others. This way, you will make the world a better place for yourself and for others. Be you, stop hating yourself and stop punishing yourself or sabotaging your health and well-being. Take heed, don't sweat for the small stuff. Small stuff should not have a place in your heart, nor in your actions or intentions. Do not let little things take over your life. Feel compassion for you and humanity. Resist the urge to be too critical. You can put things in perspective by adapting and making small changes day by day. Nurture and grow your awareness of what you are doing and what you are supposed to be doing.

It might be easier said than done, but ask yourself daily what is important to you or for you. Life seems chaotic but there is order in it at all times. What is important to you, must not be postponed. Designate where to focus your energy into, despites the many responsibilities that you have. Take care of what is important to you always and first. Reminding yourself of what is important can put back a positive organization into your life's puzzle. Kids, husband or wife, work, hobbies, secret missions and entrepreneurship can be too much to handle at the same time. But the key is to always resist being over critical in judgment or complaint about the overall life circumstances/tragedies/inequalities/injustices and asking yourself what is important to you at the moment or in the near future; with in mind that life isn't supposed to be fair. Live with compassion and goal oriented towards bettering yourself and humanity.

Role and Importance of Sample Insects and Birds

You have heard so many times that everything was connected and no single being living in the universe was separate. You have heard that you are part of the universe and also must play your role. But frankly what is your role in the universe remains a question without an answer or with so many differing answers.

In fact, nothing is out here standing by itself, by its own strength without the checks and balances of other living beings. Someone fed you and clean your poop. Someone taught you how to walk and speak by imitation. Before you could say I, there was a lot of people that made you become the I, that you jealously guarding. And if you don't pay attention while growing up and going about your life, you might ignorantly be tempted to think that you have made it through this life on your own. Forgetting that there is always someone, something somewhere that usually contributes to any success. The silent prayers and positive energies of your mother, aunts, uncles, friends, partners, casual encounters have all contributed and assisted you directly or indirectly to making you who you are claiming to be.

Now in this subject, I'm interested in insects and birds contribution to your life, to our lives and the universe. Insects like cockroaches live in majority outside of your house. Either in the bush, garden, or forest; 95% of them are staying away from your house. The remaining are the ones that visit you in your living room looking for food when you are trying to make a good impression to your guests. Beside their annoying and uninvited presence, cockroaches are useful and very important to our ecosystem.

First of all, they serve as food for a lot of species that would not have survived and carry their specific duties toward the universe to keep you alive. So in the food chain, they are used as food for birds, rats, mice, arthropods, and other insectivorous mammals. Cockroaches regulate the level of nitrogen in the universe. By providing plants and the soil the nitrogen needed for us to grow our food and for plants to grow healthy producing grains and fruits. They are recyclers, and they pretty much eat anything from dead leaf, leaf fitter to animal waste and our human waste as well. Their poops are a great nourishment for the soil and plants since they put out the nitrogen ingested from waste, as without the cockroaches' contribution, the ecosystem would have been imbalanced. They served in the continuity of the cycle always feeding the soil and our vegetal, herbal food sources. In another simple way is that you would not have enjoyed your mango, apples and rice without the help of a live cockroach nourishing, keeping the soil and plants alive.

Now let's look at the role bees play in your life and the universe. Bees help plants, trees grow, breed and produce food. Bees support the growth of the plants, trees, flowers that we use as food or shelter. They pollinate by transferring pollen between flowering plants and trees. In doing so, bees keep the cycle of life going and turning. It means that without the inputs of the bees spreading the pollen around between flowers, the plants and trees would not have produced any fruits at all since the flowers have to be pollinated first before the reproduction of the fruits. The ecosystem of plants and our source of food and economy depend greatly of the important job from the bees. In our common conception we think we just have to dig the soil, put the grain inside and water. But it takes more than that besides just some sunshine. A lot of other species small or big are helping you keep yourself alive by working without complaining for your food chain and economy not to be interrupted. 30% of the universe crops and 90% of all plants require cross-pollination to spread and grow. So the bees helped in producing your lemon, your cranberries, your melons, broccoli, mint, cilantro, strawberry, blueberry, even your herbal tea etc.

Now, what do you think of the role of the birds seating at your porch and sometimes dumping their shit on top of your newly washed car?

Birds are used for food generally. People eat them sometimes and other animals feed mostly on birds. So birds help keep the animals that prey on them from becoming numerous, thereby playing a vital role in balancing nature and the ecosystem in general. Besides, they eat insects and cockroaches too. The other most important role for us humans, is the fact that birds also help with the reproduction of plants and trees to provide us food and of course assure the continuity of the cycle. Their great services as pollinators or seed dispersers ensure the survival of the plants and trees reproductions. Taking in consideration that the plants, or trees could not carry out the process of pollination or seed dispersal without the help of the birds. And seabirds are also vital in cycling nutrients and helping to fertilize our marine ecosystems as well. Their diversities make it such that each specific bird while carrying the same duties, also has a unique inner impulse that plays a tremendous role in plants distributions, in the forest and marine health, the wildlife food chain and yours too.

Pollination is the process where the pollen for flowering plants and trees is transferred within and between plants inducing and enabling fertilization and reproduction. Bees, butterflies, wasps, birds and other animal/insects carry pollen grains from the anther to the receptive part (stigma) of the plant in order to induce pollination while flying from flower to flower.

It remains to our conscious to understand now that without the importance and role of the billions of other insects and birds including all other beings, our very life that we hold on to so dearly would not even have lived alone one full day. Without their help and them being around, your plate will be empty one day if you keep being silent about their extermination. Life is either lived orderly or chaotically. But now that you know better, act and do better.

I will end this section of the book by introducing to you the importance of the ants in our ecosystem. You will be amazed of how a wonderful job an ant has in the environment. Ants move the soil around. Ants turn the soil around. In doing so, the ants are turning and aerating the soil, facilitating and allowing water and oxygen to reach the plants and trees roots. Ants are also considered seed dispersers. Water and oxygen are crucial to any living creature and the ants have a mission to make sure the earth breathe and provide also exits for extra heat and air flow to the ground as well via their tunnels and connections of different tunnels in different locations. They are way a lot more in population size than us humans. Some researchers have estimated that it could be a more than 1.5 million ants to one man/woman. They are pretty much everywhere and live in colonies with societal organization and order. A single ant colony can have more than 20 million ants living and interacting together. You see that they could easily take us down if that was their primary mission and role in the universe. And frankly, we cannot live without them. They carry the seeds down into their tunnel and eat the nutritious elaiosomes containing within the seed. And these seeds usually sprout back up and grow new plants and trees, thereby continuing the cycle of life. They also spread around and redistribute nutrients from one space to another by moving soil particles from place to place. They improve the drainage as they build their nests/ tunnels underground improving the soil structure at the same time. Ants play a huge role of fertilizing the soil due to the fact that most of the food they store near or in their nest end up serving as nutrients for the soil; making the soil more fertile for plants and trees to grow. The bottom line is that we cannot live without the help of these small creatures that seem to be enjoying their jobs more than we love ours, taking care of everything we love while trying to avoid being stepped on by us. Next time you see an ant, you should be more thankful to their presence alone.

The Creation According to Ancient Egyptians/Kemet

First of all, it must be clear to you that Man was given birth by the mother in the beginning of the world. Man was then formed of flesh (kha) and derived his first soul from her mother's blood, the mystical parent of life. Then, the Great mother of all flesh whispered and induced the Breath of Life into his embryo to form the second soul called (Ba) or the soul of breath. It is with this primary understanding that the Ancient Egyptians concluded that the two primary elements or souls of life are Blood and Breath. And for your information, the Ba (your second soul) breathes as well. Now that I'm going to inform you that there are seven souls in each man/woman, I'll be proceeding with the remaining five's and their requirements, since you know already about the kha and the Ba:

- The Third Soul (Khabs) is the astral shade or shadow soul. It envelops the second soul (Ba) in a form of visible light like a cover or a veil. The light is visible but not tangible. The third soul is represented and compared to an eclipse like sunshade. It is that soul that when lost/loss, the spirit doctor has to go find it and retrieve it before the shadow soul crosses over, where it becomes almost impossible to intercede.

- The Fourth Soul (Akhu) is a form of mind giving the man/woman the ability and possibility to memorize or to remember. The ability to perceive too is part and makes up the qualities of the fourth soul. That's also why a loss of memory is considered a loss of a soul. Absence of mind is another form of losing one's soul too.
- The Fifth Soul (Seb) is the animal soul. It is also considered the ancestral soul. The animal soul only descends to man/woman not until puberty. Upon puberty only that anyone can have access to the fifth soul.
- The Sixth Soul (Putah) is the first intellectual father, the intellectual soul. The soul that brings and adds wisdom to the first intellect. It is the soul that is identified as Buddha in India, the god Ptah, the opener in Egypt, Buddhi in Hindu or lord of the sixth creation. And finally,
- The Seventh Soul (Atmu) is the divine and the eternal soul. It is the Individualized creative soul that represents the Eternal, signifying that this particular soul has reached godhood, fatherhood, Atmu or Atma. In that stage of spiritual growth,

the person once the seventh' soul is attained becomes everlasting and created forever, reaching the status of sole one God without change after culminating and reaching Its highest development with the Eighth and final soul. Mystically, the person's becomes the re-born Sun, the re-born Spirit or glorified Ghost of Man or simply a born-again, raised from the dead or if you prefer, resurrected or a star with eight points. Consequently, the three witnesses or the three trinity are Spirit, water and Blood. And the three are in agreement.

Sample Names of God's Worshiped and Forgotten?

The point of this paragraph is to have you take it easy on yourself when it comes to what you portray or think is God. You would need to be open minded as, if you hold on dearly to your beliefs and traditions, you might miss the point. At the end, what you need to understand about God is to realize that once you give God a name, it immediately loses its value and sanctity, because you have dragged God down to your small minded ways of living in society by names. And I think that we are screwed if God was a person that changes names like a time clock; since it might not be unusual for the same God to be called by different names. Anyway here are few names of God's that are worshiped or been worshiped: Ra, Amon, Isis, Horus, Osiris, Aten, Montu, Amun-Ra, Zeus, Ashur, Ishtar, Nabu, Tiamat, Marduk, Sammuha, Kubaba, Inanna, Utu, Enki, Isumud, Anunnaki, Chthnic, Igigi, Enlil, Astarte, Atargatis, Aglibol, Baalshamin, Palmyra, Bes, Humban, Hutran, Inshushinak, Inzak, Lagamal, Ishmekerab, Malakbel, Meskilak, Muati, Nahhunte, Napir, Pienenkir, Lahamun, Manzat, Ruhurater, kilahsupir, Tirutir,

Siyasum, Narunte, Niarzina, Simut, Yahweh, El, Elohim, El Shaddai, Yah, Yarhibol, Benum, Hecate, Diana, Juno, Metis, Ceres, Cybele, Cora, Phoebe, Athena, Aurora, Flora, Freya, Luna, Selena, Thalia, Aine, Devi, Lakshmi, Niamh, Momus, Morpheus, Nereus, Notus, Oceanus, Pallas, Nanna, Sedna, Wakan Tanka, Glooscap, Coyote, Gitche Manitou, Kokopelli, Tlaloc, AsdzaaNadleehe, Manitou, Igaluk, Pachamama, Xiuhtecuhtli, Tonatiuh, Tezcatlipoca, Huitzilopochtli, Ahone, Torngarsuk, Pinga, Azeban, Atahensic, Tlazolteotl, Ometeotl, Coatlicue, Xolotl, Jupiter, Mars, Neptune, Venus, Mercury, Miverna, Apollo, Vulcan, Pluto, Saturn, Vesta, Cupid, Janus, Proserpina, Victoria, Faunus, Demeter, Poseidon, Fortuna, Sol, Terra, Hera, Aphrodite, Hermes, Artemis, Athena, Hephaestus, Poseidon, Ares, Hades, Dionysus, Hestia, Persephone, Eros, Helios, Cronus, Rhea, Gaia, Nyx, Atlas, Ascleplus, Hou Yi, Shangdi, Chiyou, Pangu, Chang'e, Guanyin, Sun Wukong, Nezha, CaiShen, Doumu, Dragon, GuangZeZun Wang, ZaoShen, Cao Guojiu , Amaterasu, Benzaiten, Ebisu, Daikokuten, Izanami, Izanagi, Jurojin, Fukurokuju, Vaisravana, Ame-no-Uzume, Kagutsuchi, Amitabha, lnari, Fujin, Hachiman, Ksitigarbha, Ninigi-no-Mikoto, Kojin, Guanyin, Acala, Amatsumikaboshi, Raijin, Oyamatsumi, Watatsumi, Inti, Viracocha, Manco-Capac, Chantico, Huixtocihuatl, Malinalxochitl, Itzpapalotl, Chasa, Ixcacao, Mayahuel, Xochimilco, AsaseYaa, Coyolxauhqui, Temazcalteci,

Eingana, Teteoinnan, Gaulchovang, Aluna, Sai-Tana, Gauteovan, His, Hers, Mma, Juya, Dobeiba, Fura-Chogua, Dabeiba, Bachue, Chuchabiba, Chia, Huitaca, Nana Dumat, Umina, Pachamama, Kuma, Amana, Chagra mama, Oya, Olorun, Shango, Yemaja, Obatala, Aberewa, Aja, Ala, Amma, AsaaseAfua, Faro, Gbadu, Inkosazana, Kitaka, Mamlambo, Mawu-Lisa, MbabaMwanaWaresa, Majaji, Nkwa, Obba, Olokun, Oshun, Woyengi, Abassi, Asis, Bemba, Chiuta, Deng, En-Kai, Eshu, Gulu, Gurzil, Ibeji, Imana, Banyarwanda, Kanu, Katonda, Lesa, Mulungu, Nyame, Ogun, Sagbata, Tore, Tororut, Unkulunkulu, Waka, Zanahary, Yala, Tel, Ngai, Akongo, Mawu, Bore-Bore, Yatta, Ondo, Wuro, Hathor, Bastet, Thoth, Anubis, Ptah, Aker, Anhur, Atum, Bennu, Geb, Hapi, Khepri, Khnum, Khnemu, Khonsu, Maahes, Montu, Nefertum, Nemty, Neper, Set, Shu, Sobek, Sopdu, Wadj-wer, Amunet, Anuket, Bastet, Bat, Heqet, hesat, Imentet, Ma'at, Menhit, Mut, Neith, Nut, Nekhbet, Nepit, Pakhet, Renenutet, Satet, Sekhmet, Tefnut, Wadjet, Wosret, Uatchit, Ganesha, Shiva, Rama, Brahma, Kali, Krishna, Durga, Kartikeya, Hanuman, Vishnu, Indra, Varuna, Agni, Saraswati, Lakshmi, Vayu, Parvati, Surya, Prajapati, Ayyappan, Vamana, Matsya, Varahi, Kamakshi, Jehovah, El Shaddai, El Elyon, Adonai, Qanna, Gnostic Christ, Jesus Christ, Chistus, Pharaoh, Allah, Elat, Eloha, Alla, Allahu, Allaha etc.

If the name you call your God is not here, there are so many names that I almost gotten tired of writing because of their different spelling, I had to focus on getting the names right. Now, are the names really important? Knowing that most of these names are not the original spellings or sound or pronunciation from their beginning. I'm also sure that all those people that have worshiped these different God's in their respective time frame and year, were expecting for salvation and a ticket to heaven. And we lacked the proof to confirm if all the God's were worshiped willingly without intimidation or persecutions.

The only question that remains is: aren't they talking about the same God? Unless you are only interested in worshiping the individuals, instead of the presence and essence in them; the God particles, their way of life and the positive changes they contributed to humanity?

So if you were hoping to show up on heaven and claim that you belong to this God and give the God's name, don't be surprised when the gate keeper tells you that nobody respond to that god name there. Simply because each one of them has become one with the One Consciousness thereby not separated from each-others. Then Christus whom has been executed by Pilate in the first century A.D. told Thomas that Salvation consists of Self-Knowledge. Christus was responsible for disturbances or disturbing the order established/imposed by the Romains in the

Hebrew faith community in Rome because on the first century no-one was called Jew yet.

Every God's or Master name up there is telling you that you must know thyself (yourself) first, that way your yes will be yes and your no will be no; and you will then be able to detect false teachers/preachers. Remember that your History is old and the History of the world is old as well. People migrate, tribes migrate, cities, countries, continents, regions change names, landscapes, societal traditions; and all it takes is a change of customs from only three generations and you might no longer recognized an old tradition, culture, religion based on the recent actual facts in comparison. The land remains there, but the people living in that land might be completely different in skin colors, different way of life and different religion or culture etc. For example, ancient Greeks are different from the modern Greeks; ancient Egyptians/ Kemet are different from our modern Egyptians; ancient Israelites are different from our modern Israelites; ancient Palestinians are different from our modern Palestinians; ancient Italians are different from our modern Italians, ancient Romans, ancient Syrians are also different from our modern Syrians and so forth. Just like in some parts of North Africa is now called middle East, but in ancient times the actual location of Israel, Palestine, Greece, Italy, France, Spain, India, china, America and pretty much everywhere in the world were all populated under one single race that we call black-people today. Therefore, all and most God's names embedded the same spirit and origin only with a different name as time went by. So, just focus on getting yourself better and knowing your own self because you might not even know that the sky and the stars make music to you; that the Sun and the Moon praise you; even the gods sing to you. Find your voice and play your own music that is missing in your music-body in order to realign your body musical frequency. Through the trueness and sincerity of your own voice, you are then healed and resurrected. As above, so below. Your ancestors always knew that there is a rise and always a fall to everything and everything at the same time has a tide, a wave, a frequency, a force. The solution to survive the swing of the pendulum is through neutralization because as you know the pendulum always swings back and forth. Always remember that every kid including you, is born with his own music and with his own voice. Find the keynote to your voice and you will be healed. You are the measure of all things that exists including the gods, stars, moons, suns and the other billions of planets. Therefore, you are co-partner of the other Beings just as above so below. The story of the universe and in the universe are your story and the story of all of us including time and space; frequencies and energy just like you and me. So we all speak the universe language which is based on energy, frequency and form. That is the only way to understanding the universe and yourself. Think frequency, think energy, and think vibration, sound and form concludes the universal code. The whole universe is singing and is built on harmonies; together with you singing along in One Song. You are a complete mature being that have already reached his/her highest evolution, evolvement and it is time to acknowledge that truth and start acting like a full being entitled to this universe just like your other partners residing in different planets and dimensions.

Short History of Africans and African Descents Before the Greek Invasion

I will begin this chapter with a quotation from one of the most prominent Black Egyptologist. His great works and research have put back the Africans past civilization into the world attention. For him, Africa was truly the cradle of almost all the civilizations throughout the world. Of the name of Pr. Cheikh Anta Diop, he stated: "Far from being a self-indulgent fixation on the past, the examination of ancient Egypt is our wisest option if we intend to plan and create our cultural future."

Glancing back into our past History and Culture, Sirius was the focus of the Egyptian life and societal order. It is the Star whose sight brings joy and celebration for everyone including the rich, the poor, the nobles and the citizen lambda. It disappears below the horizon once a year for a period of seventy days and reappears in mid-summer for another seventy days. Each time Sirius shows up, it is a beginning of a new cycle and by the middle of every April, Sirius becomes no visible until the summer. It can even be seen in bright day light with a telescope with an aperture of 12mm. The Star Sirius rises once every 365 days but every 1461 years its rising coincides with the rising of the Sun making the Sun and Sirius rising together at the same time every 1461 years. The Star Sirius is the center of our world religions as well. It was the center of the Egyptians/ Kemet religion. The Kemet have come to understand over time that Sirius/Sopdet is the power behind the Sun and the Spiritual Body of the Sun. Sirius is also the brightest Star in our Galaxy. In fact on July 19th 2020, it was the Kemet New Year; it was the date Sopdet reappeared on the eastern horizon after 70 days long absence and it is usually the day the Nile began to flood. Sirius/Sopdet was associated with Aset, in which the Greeks later called Isis including the Romans but the Romans would change the name with the creation of Christianity to Mary/Madonna whom you now know to be the mother of Jesus Christ. And Aset/Isis/Mary are considered the mother goddess of the Earth who are parts of the trinity. In fact, Sirius is a Greek word and the Egyptians called it Sopdet if you were probably wondering why I associated the word "Sopdet" next to Sirius. The word Egypt is also Greek and the real name is Kemet, the land of black people or black land.

Sopdet is located farther east and farther south than the second brightest star Rigel even though both might be similar in appearance but Sopdet/Sirius is the brighter; brighter than all the other stars in our galaxy including the Sun. Besides, the star Rigel is even 33 times greater than our Sun and radiates 23,000 times more light than our Sun; and Bellatrix takes the third brightest star in the Zodiac.

Since, it looks like we cannot talk about Sirius/Sopdet without brushing over the trinity of our world's religions; the original trinity is of the Kemet's which is Ausar/ Usir, Aset, and Heru. And of course the Greeks imitate it by changing the names to be Osiris, Isis, and Horus; that the Romans would later transformed to Father, Son, and the Holly Spirit. The main substance and ideology remain the same except the names. If you take a look of the story of Heru, Horus and Jesus Christ, they are identical from the beginning to the end which implies a sophisticated plagiarism or it could be that names don't really matters while the substance behind the names is the most important aspect. Maybe, it is the location of the most important Stars in our Galaxies that it is all about? May be instead of focusing on names, you should just take a look in another direction that is Orion or Sah.

Orion was called by the Kemet's Sah and was considered to represent Ausar/Usir. Later called by the Greeks Orion and assimilated to represent Osiris. And Sah/Orion will be visible in the night sky for a period of seventy days (70) in the Northern Hemisphere since Sah/ Orion is mostly a winter constellation of the northern region of the planet earth. By the way, the Great pyramid of the Kemet now in Egypt is in alignment with Sirius/ Sopdet and the Orion belt, emphasizing how relevant and important these Stars represented for the Kemets. And of course, every time Sirius/Sopdet is set to Rise, it must be announced by the three Men/Magi/Stars or the three Marys/ or the three wise Men readapted within the Bible called Mintaka, Alnilam, and Alnitak in the belt of Orion/Sah which points directly to Osiris/Ausar' Star in the East, Sirius/Sopdet, as a sign of his birth. Since then, the Kemets have linked their Solar Calendar based on the Heliacal rising of Sopdet/Sirius at the eastern horizon in order to keep up with the Calendar; and each time that the star appears, it is usually the day the Nile begins to flood signaling the First season called Akhet. Take note that the word Akhet means Flood or Inundation.

Thanks to Sirius/Sopdet, the Kemets knew then that there is a period of precession of the Equinoxes every 25,920 years. And following the precession, a world cataclysm always happens that literally wipe out all or almost all existence including humans, animals and vegetal lives. In doing so, it changes the world landscape for a new world. And between the cycles, there are periodic cataclysms included within the full cycle of the 25,920 years that are purely independent of anyone's impulse or global karma. It would happens regardless if everyone on earth is living life as a saint. They were well aware of the 365 days cycle completing a full year by observing the movement of the earth and of the Sun. The Kemets observed that a day makes 24 hours and earth turns around the Sun completely every day and it is only after turning for 365 days that the Sun turns Ones in its own orbit. Our ancients/ancestors stated that after the completion of the 25,920 years, the gods will reappear on earth to set the new impulse and sense of future direction in line accordingly to divine purpose for mankind to follow as a road map. They warned us that those gods will not be born from any intercourse or sex as we know of a male and a female having sex to make a baby or with a fantasy spirit. The gods will self-project and self-create themselves without no-one's involvement. The gods will begin the cycle until they are replaced by semi-divine kings/queens and leaders followed by the era of heroes and spiritual adepts completing the order of how the universe works through its own inbuilt cycles. After the said three cycles, men and women will be left on their own to choose their own leaders and eventually complete the fourth cycle by becoming lovers of themselves and comfortable in social disorder/immorality.

So, the heliacal rising of Sirius/Sopdet at the horizon was very crucial even for a brief time because of its reliance in keeping up with the calendar. In those days, the Kemets have divided the year into three seasons, in which each season is four months long. The first season is called Akhet that means Flood or Inundation. The names of each of the four months during the first season are Teth, Menhet, Hwt-Hrw, and Ka-Hr-Ka. Followed by the second season called Proyet which means Emergence/

Growing. Sf-Bdt, Redh Wer, Redh Neds, and Renwet are the months throughout the second season. And finally the third season called Shomu that means Low Water/ Harvest throughout the last four months; that are called Hnsw, Hnt-Htj, Ipt-Hmt, and Wep-Renpet. The month was called Abed, the days Heru and the solar year Renpet. This solar calendar was used for daily social life in which one week was ten days and three weeks make one month totaling thirty days. The workweek was nine straight days and one day to rest. After the three seasons that totaled 360 days, the remaining five days was for holy days celebrating the New Year. Five days was set to celebrate the gods/goddesses and the coming of the New Year. Please note that the names of the different months, days and years may have changed over the years depending on the dynasty era.

Another aspect to underscore when talking about the Star Sirius/Sopdet is that it announces the coming of the savior. And the savior was Ausar/Usir, then Osiris. Behold, the pyramids Texts says: "The coming of Ausar/Osiris, the savior of the Kemet was "the Star in the East" because when Sopdet/Sirius rises with the Sun, or "heliacally", life along the Nile becomes abundant and everything starts growing and flourishing; thereby rejuvenating life at the Nile. In this note, you must now understand that Osiris/ Ausar is Orion as the Pyramid texts continued as "He has come as Orion/Sah. Osiris/Ausar has come as Orion."

With those representations Sirius and Orion or Sopdet and Sah, Isis and Osiris or Aset and Ausar.

So the Nile depended on that greatly and each time, Osiris/Ausar is born, life comes back at the Nile and it was called for a celebration annually as a big event since it was set to renew the land again. In the First Dynasty of the Kemet (c.3100B.C) it is said on a carved small ivory that "Sopdet/Sirius is the opener of the Year's Flood." And again the pyramid Texts (c.2200B.C.) continued "It is Sopdet/Sirius, the beloved daughter (of Ra, the Sun-god), who prepares yearly sustenance (the flood for you in her name of 'year')." It is amazing that in some more than 5000 years ago, the Star in the East gave birth to the Kemet/Egyptian Messiah thousands of years before the Christian era of course with Jesus Christ as their savior. And each Resurrection was due to Sopdet-Sirius/Isis-Aset waking up Ausar/Osiris from the dead. If you remember the story of Isis-Osiris, it is said that Isis (Osiris' wife) found the fourteen pieces of Osiris (Isis's husband) scattered throughout Egypt when Seth, Osiris' brother killed and dismantled him. The story continued with Isis-Aset reassembling Osiris dismembered body parts back together to bring him back to life. And after bringing him back to life with her Magic Powers, she conceived a divine and supernatural child with him that is called Heru, Horus, later called Jesus-Christ by Christians. Therefore, the rise of Sirius/Sopdet-Isis means the beginning of the summer solstice announcing the coming of Osiris/Ausar bringing abundance. And the rising of Orion which is Osiris, with the three Kings/ three stars/ three wise-men pointing means the end of the flooding, going towards the winter solstice announcing the birth of the savior child Heru, Horus, Jesus-Christ.

The pyramid Text 593:1636b/M206 states that: "Heru, Horus, and now Jesus the pointed has come forth from thee, in his name "Heru, Horus, Jesus, who is in Sirius/ Sopdet." Which would come to mean that it is the Sun rising with Sirius, the Sun in Sirius meaning Horus in Sirius making the birth of Heru/Horus/Jesus associated with the Star in the East. Consequently, the three Kings point to the Star in the East, which the Star in the East in turn announces the coming of the savior that is the rising/ birth of the Sun; and the Sun is nothing else but what is known as Heru, Horus, Jesus, in our religious mythology. Remember here that the three kings are the representation of the Orion belt, the three stars (Mintaka, Alnitak, Alnilam) known as the Hunter's belt. In winter, right before the annual birth and rise of the Sun, it happened or coincided right after the three kings in the belt of Orion have pointed to Sirius at night, concluding here that Heru is the Sun, Horus is the Sun and lately Jesus is the Sun. Therefore, the world's religions rested all on this Astro-theologic facts and knowledge given by the Universe itself. It is news to me too as I'm finding out that we are really all screwed up when it comes to knowledge, because I would not have even come across this piece of information if I was not doing my own research; and not till after more than ten years of consistent writings and readings. So my friends, do your own research also and see the truth through your own eyes and inner-insight.

At the Beginning, Earth was Without a Moon

During my many readings and research, I came across some records that maintained that there was actually a period on earth where earth was without a moon. Yes you read it right; earth moon was not attached to earth from the beginning. At this point, all we have is past written records stating that far far back in our earthly existence, we only had the Sun as light on days and stars at night. I'm still figuring out how were the nights at those days like?

So, if earth did not have a moon, when and how did that moon event took place?

Aristotle mentioned in one his writings that "Arcadia before it was inhabited by the Hellenes, Arcadia had a population of Pelasgians. And that those aborigines lived there and occupied the land already way before there was even a moon in the sky above the earth. And because of that, and they were called Proselenes."

Appollonius of Rhodes, Plutarch, Ovid, Lucian, all in their writings records that Arcadia or the Arcadians were on earth living for a long time prior to earth suddenly having a moon. I guess no-one can prove it or disprove the idea or the fact that earth was indeed at the beginning without moon; only with a Sun and Stars. Democritus and Anaxagoras actually taught in schools too that there was a time when the earth was without a Moon.

In some oral traditions across the globe, the Indians of Bogota Highlands in the eastern cordilleras of Colombia said and confirmed that some of their ancestors lived on earth before there was a moon. As a reminiscence, those tribes would gather and remember those ancient past days of their ancestor having existed on earth way before it was a moon. And in some account of the Zulu tribe, there is also a memory of an earth without a moon; and that according to one of the Zulu tribe priest/Shaman, the moon appears to be hallow like an egg that has had its yoke taken out. It was also heard mentioned by a tribesmen of Chibchas "in the earliest times, when the moon was not yet in the heavens."

In addition, the Kalevala of the Finns recalls indeed a time "when the moon was placed in orbit". (Rune III.35). The ible at some point mentioned or gave an account of an earth existing with inhabitants without a moon yet. Some older and earlier writing in the Bible suggested a period where the moon was not. On Job 25:5 before it was taken out is read as follow: The grandeur of the Lord who "makes peace in the heights" is praised and (the time is mentioned) "before [there was] a moon and it did not shine". And in Psalm 72:5 it is said also "thou was feared since [the time of] the Sun and before [the time of] the moon, a generation of generations."

At the end of the day, one thing I retain here is that I do not know and that there are things and events in ancient past that will blow your mind and insult your intelligence. What do you make of written records of a moon that was born before your time anyway and actually picture an earth without it? The moon is not just randomly placed there, because it lines up with the Sun perfectly that in full lunar Eclipse, the moon becomes as the same size as the Sun. when in truth, the Sun is way bigger than it. And the diameter of the said moon times 108 is the distance between earth and moon. Whoever or the people or the forces or the natural phenomena, responsible for locking the moon with our earth are excellent in astronomy, mathematics, physics, and a lot magic or knowledge of the energy and matter of the universe. Don't forget that the same very moon dictates also our weather, days, our well-being and our time.

To conclude this section of the book, let me add you some ammunition for your soul surviving mission. The Olmec discovered America; not Columbus. A logical question comes to my mind. Who else discovered America before the Olmec when earth was potentially without a moon at some point of human existence? The first emperor of China Fu-Si is said to be African and the first pharaoh of Egypt NARMER was also black-skinned/

African. Moses was married to Zipporah and Jesus Christ to Marie Magdalene that were both African princesses including both themselves. Amos (a black ancestor) gave Mathematics to the world. Thoth, another black ancestor was the inventor of writing, the creator of languages, and the adviser of the gods including being the representative of the sun god, Ra. Amenhotep, an ancient Egyptian/Kemet is the father of Medicine. You must cherish your melanin, your blackness and be proud of it, because it is the Melanin that gives you your strength, your inner compassion and access to the Highest Consciousness ever possible to mankind. Thanks to your Melanin, you cannot get skin cancer and your wounds heal faster too. You have survived all of the world atrocities century after century thanks to the greatness of your melanin that always sustains you and helps you easily shake-off the pains and suffering afflicted to you and your ancestors. Let the geneticists confirm that to you in the global patterns of linkage disequilibrium at the CD4 locus and modern human origins (1996). While testing DNA series, the geneticists learned that Africans have the highest number as follow: the Orangutan is 3 DNA series, the Gorilla is 4 DNA series, the chimpanzee is 5 DNA series; all whites and non-blacks have 6 DNA series and Black-Skinned people (Africans) have 9 DNA series. That's one of the unfortunate reasons Melanin and Black Skins are the most precious and the most trafficked around the world.

At the end, the only thing I have control on is me; and the best time is your present time. Live it and experience every little bit of it. Remain focus and remind yourself that one solar day is 24 hours and one divine day is 360 days of human life. Develop and open your third eye to be able to heal yourself and your loved ones. Before you proceed to the next paragraph, it is important to note that there is a speculation that the Mayans actually disappeared and they may have ascended to a different dimension or went underground; because there is an under-earth within earth itself called the Underworld. In that Underworld, behold, there are rivers, trees, gardens, birds as well. So, the next time someone tells you that he/she has seen a man/woman with a bird like head, or snake like head, please don't be quick to dismiss the person because it might be true and is actually a fact just like there are talking trees.

Numbers Governing the Universe Inside Out

In the Mayan calendar, it is mentioned that it takes 144.000 days for the time of the new beginning as part of the time cycle. At the same token, the same 144.000 is also mentioned in the Bible referring to 144.000 chosen ones that will be redeemed prior to the time of apocalypse. I should remind you that the true definition of apocalypse is new beginning as well. The Ancient Egyptians have also built the Great Pyramid of Giza in North Africa with a total of 144.000 smooth pieces of stones. Considering that each Stone used for the construction of the pyramid weight 2.5 tons each, the number of the stone must also bear a great significance knowing that there is a planetary alignment with the said pyramid of Giza and the Orion belt that only happens once every 2773 years.

Another significant number is the natural tuning of the universe which is 432 Hz (Hertz). It is the natural frequency of the universe that resonates within a golden ratio automatically connecting every single cell within each person's body, animal, plants and minerals putting all of us in harmony with each other including the universe itself; and consequently to the Supreme Being commonly called God the unseen. It is for this reason that musicians and ancient civilizations have all tuned their instrument to 432 Hz. The number 432 Hz is in harmony with natural life rhythm on earth including earth itself as 432 Hz is also considered to be the heartbeat of mother earth. You are feeling this earth heartbeat at every single second that passes. We have 24 hours divided into two known names as days and nights sharing 12 hours each a piece. The number 432 comes into play again as we have 432.000 seconds in each 12 hours making a total of 864.000 seconds in a full day. From now on, look around yourself and notice what's there in the universe to know.

Now, I will attempt to make this paragraph more fascinating. When you divide 144.000 by 432, it gives you a series of three's (333.33333333) and you might have learn in high school that three (3) is the first number that forms a geometrical figure known as the triangle. It was even considered in past civilizations as the true number as far as it is the number of the divine; and a sacred number in many religions as well or simply the trinity. It is the number that completes the single digit number in the decimal system when put in square; 3 square gives 9 followed by 10 and 3 plus 3 totals 6; making 3,6,9 a magic constant of the 9 times 9 magic square and the n-queens problem for n=9. In talking about how special the number three is, these numbers 33.3 thirteen times (33.3x13) give a sum of

432.9. And 432.9 is the number harmonizing the people, the plants and the universe all inclusive. It is once said that the number 3, 6, 9, holds the key to the universe and might be a vector from the third to the fourth dimension that influences earthly manifestations too.

Let's take a look at our Sun. It seemingly rises and sets because of the earth rotating on its axis 24 hours daily. The truth is, as the Earth rotates towards the east, it actually looks like the Sun itself is moving west. In fact, the Sun has not moved not even a bit. It is our planet earth that is moving and going away in rotation around in from east to west on its own axis. This is part of number governing the universe movement as during the earth rotation daily, as your town turns towards the Sun and the light of the Sun illuminate your town, it looks like the Sun is rising in the east. And when your very town begins to leave the sun light and enter into darkness, it now appears that the same Sun is now setting in the west. Half the time when the Sun is in your town, it is daytime and night time on the other side. When it is night time on your side of the town, then it is day time on the other side. The same goes with our moon. We see it through the reflection of our Sun based on the Sun reflecting its own light to the moon;

and only when the moon light is on our side of town or earth. Because this time around it is the moon now that is orbiting and going around earth and your town. That's why you can even see the moon from your town in a bright day light. Numbers do not lie and it is and has been like that from generations to this generation.

The Real Danger of Not Detoxing Periodically

For few, the idea of detox looks appealing and attractive and for others it is a new concept or something that is not mandatory. Detoxing is an important aspect of life and in any living being, human life included. It has been mandated centuries before us and will still remain relevant for the coming years. Detoxing may take a lot of forms: mental, physical and spiritual as far as human life is concerned. Some cultures require a detox every 90 days, some every three month or spaced out in between weeks depending of your life style and habits. When you chew food in your month and swallow, you still have some left-over food stock within your teeth, at the bottom of your tongue including your throat and almost every aspect of the digestive process combined. Did you know that your small intestine alone measure about over twenty feet or more than seven meters on average and your large intestines about five feet or 1.5 meters?

Those little left over foods will accumulate over time causing blockages, mucus within the digestive systems to a certain degree to cause sickness, emotional disturbance, hormones chemical unbalances, stress, constipation, diarrhea; and that falls under the physical detox to say the least.

A mental detox is also recommended in order to target the subconscious of the individual since a man is no less or more than what he or she thinks and thinks of himself. The mental detox is a must for each individual hoping to be free from mental slavery, from societal intoxication, from prejudices and common false beliefs. Wrong things that have been taught to you and your far family need to be corrected with the right knowledge and history. Those descending directly or indirectly from families that have been forced to slavery, oppression, colonization, and systemic discrimination must do immediately a mental detox to break the chains of bondages. Regardless of which category you fall in, consider yourself that your mind and the minds you inherited from your ancestors have been corrupted and contain a bunch of toxic and self-incriminating knowledge and habits.

An aura cleansing is mandatory as well as a spiritual detox including realigning all the chakras for optimum circulation of the energy within and enlightenment. Above all, meditation, exercising daily, plant based diet, mucus-less diet and breath control, martial arts, dance, herbs, constructive and educative knowledge and music are the most universal ways to address most and all of the above detox recommendations. You should see that kids and elderly people follow the recommendation since it will increase the family solidarity, love and loyalty. Most people have difficulty holding a relationship or caring for their family members unconditionally due to the fact that they are not detoxing neither body, neither mind nor spirit. I should warn you that such people would most likely contaminate every single person they come into contact energetically even in habits and emotions, especially during sexual intimacy. Have you heard this saying; "show me your friends and I might know who you are"? In this context, it is the magnetic spheres of each being that will interfere and interact with each other, following a discharge and exchange of energies, thoughts, feelings, sensations, emotions and actions and deeds even karma. Consequently, when exposed for a long time to people that have a dirty aura, dirty mind, dirty impulse and thinking, twisted chakras, sleepy soul, if you don't take guard, it could even have an impact in the way your atoms are arranged within each other; that when rearranged differently in a negative way accordingly and relatively, it will make you sick and lower your vibration levels, your frequency levels and your energy level. You know we are made of atoms that came from the stars themselves out of star dust which is Carbon. Just for your information, Carbon is composed of six (6) Protons, six (6) Neutrons and six (6) Electrons. If you are familiar with the number 666, then you may know now that it is the number of the original beginning;

not the number of no beast by coincidence unless you are the one being portrayed as the beast. By the way, the most common elements in intelligent beings including us human are hydrogen, oxygen, carbon, nitrogen; and in the universe we can add helium that is inert.

At the end of the day, your oppressor have control over nothing but your mind, therefore, it is a must that you reclaim your subconscious mind, and that's the only way you will become a real free man/woman equally able to speak, protect and stand for yourself and capable of saying what is right and best for you and yours. Even if this would mean breathing like a fish in the water; fish breathe by taking the water into their mouths and forcing it out through the grill passages. Exactly like deep breathing which is inhale and exhale. Mind you that there is still gravity even in the water (ocean, lake, river etc.) even though water has more weight in proportion than the air you are breathing now. You must detox your body, your mind and even your spirit periodically because the blood within you is also subject to gravity. The only reason your blood is not dropping low to your feet, is because your heart keeps pumping blood throughout your whole body. When your heart stops, the same blood falls down back to your feet due to the blood weight pulled by gravity. Remain focus at all times, endure if you must, but at the end, control your mind, emotions, and your spirit will be strong and sharp like a shiny knife.

Energy and Its Ramifcation's to Life

Energy is the life force of any living being. Rocks have energy and need energy. Trees have energy and need energy. Animals have energy and need energy; and humans too have energy and need energy. Everything is energy and at the same time need energy to survive daily or when extremely needed. I wish I could talk about other beings beside humans. If only and when I know what to say about others, I will not hesitate. Retain this fact that at every level of life anywhere in our worlds known and unknown, we all use and need energy to continue life regardless of the dimensions. For the moment, what I found out is that each human being has different types of energy. You can try to name those types but at the end of the day, we have our present or actual energy that can be spent for our daily lives. We constantly need energy at all times. You also have your inherited energy which is the one you are born with. Both different sources of energies are available to you. Either way, you have to burn some type of energy to live daily. When you are no longer able to satisfy the energy needs from your exterior life, you tap into your inherited energy to keep providing energy to your body, mind and spirit need. Your exterior life will mean what you eat, drink, think, desire, wish, love etc.; whatever usage of your energy daily will still need energy and when needed to be replaced and continuously be fed. That's why when you the individual fails to have enough needed energy, the person will then turn to tapping into his/her inherited energy. Some of us tap into our inherited energy sooner than others depending of each individual life circumstances. And when that happened, we may experience aging or premature aging, graying, muscles and/or joint stiffness, arthritis, heart disease, Alzheimer etc. Energy is important for life and is needed every day, every minute and every second. Therefore, energy must be replenished on daily basis with proper diet, nutrients, exercise, meditation, walking and everything else that will keep your life going in a positive way. Eat right, think right, breathe right and exercise right; this way you might have added couple of seconds, minutes or hours to your life span.

Meridians are Your Body Energy Roadmap

Meridians are the channels where the energy of the body is carried to from point A to point B throughout the whole body. The meridians have their specific route like a road map that is invisible to a naked eye so to speak. Energy must be understood as the body actual vital force that gives strength and dynamism to the person's body. I understand that most people are not familiar with the concept of the energetic anatomy that all beings possess within the body, but it is crucial for you to know. You might have heard at some point that you have your blood flows within your body following its own road map called the vessels. Just like blood flows through the vessels, your body energy also runs through your meridians. For information purposes, you should know the nerves of your body carry your body's sensory information through its specific route and the Autonomic Nervous System (ANS) which is part of your nervous system monitor and regulates the chemical communication network system such as your heart beat, blood pressure, digestion and urination, your whole body's internal environment; So your body energy also has pathways which are the meridians. The ANS is itself regulated by the hypothalamus.

In fact studies have been conducted surrounding the existence of such meridians and when a CT scan was performed in a person's body, it reveals indeed that there is an existence of such meridians carrying your body energy. It is considered a map of acupuncture points in the body and that meridian lines are just like a duck system within the body in which the energy of the body flows through.

This piece of knowledge should be interesting to you as you can now pay attention to how your body energy moves within your body. And when we are talking about a system that transports energy, chances are that there will be times when the road that facilitates the passages of energy gets blocked or hit a red light or get narrowed subsequently causing a decrease or halt of energy that was supposed to be carried to your organs and body. When someone's meridians get blocked or narrowed, the energy distribution relatively to your body reduces or stops the energy from moving and circulating. In this situation, the flow of energy must be restored promptly for the person to continue enjoying health, joy, peace, lack of anxiety, stress etc. you will get sick, weak, paranoid, and a lot more undesirable effect to your health including emotional disturbance and spiritually not feeling grounded.

According to Ancient knowledge and now proven in our modern times, there are twelve (12) Main Meridians within each human body and each meridian correspond to a specific human major organ. We have the stomach meridian, the spleen meridian, the heart meridian, the lung meridian, the liver meridian, the pericardium meridian, the bladder meridian and of course the kidney meridians, the gallbladder meridian, the small intestine meridian, the large intestines meridian, including the triple burner meridian. The triple burner that is the hallow space inside the trunk regulates the body temperature by the way and is known of today's science as the trunk.

By now, it should be clear to you that each meridian that is linked to a specific organ is not there by mistake from the maker of mankind. The human body functions just like your computer, iPhone or simply like a machine built with component and a software that works without fail based on why and how it was built for. The human body is by far one of the most sophisticated machine compared to any man-made computer and other artificial intelligence. It should not surprise you any longer that each meridian carries many life-saving and essential bodily function that overall guarantee your well-being at all time and at any place. Such as providing your body with energy for its movement. In fact, meridians are also responsible for your muscles to be furnished in energy. Your muscles get their energy through each corresponding meridian. Because each meridian organ corresponds at the same time and location to a muscle group. Just to name a few example, the kidneys are associated with your lower back muscles and the small intestine to your quadriceps and abdominal muscles.

Have you heard about yin and yang, also known as the duality in life? Like all things existing within the universe have their opposing forces. Yin, yang is also known as for example cold and hot, life and death and so on. In your body also, there is a yin, and a yang system built within you to keep you balanced and healthy. There are six yin and six yang that the total makes your twelve meridians that are each paired three by three linking them organs by organs. It goes like this; three yin meridians (heart, lung and pericardium) linking in the same order three yang meridians that are the (small intestine, the large intestine and san Jiao) of the arm. Note here that the pericardium is a membrane or a thin sac that envelops and surrounds the heart itself. It protects and lubricates your heart and keeps your heart in place within your chest. Heart problems are possibly linked to that membrane or thin sac being enflamed or filled with fluid and in some cases when the membrane gets too thin or thinner, it slows or stops the flow of energy and vital nutrients.

The other three yin meridians that are the (liver, the kidney and the spleen) also linked order by order the remaining three yang meridians known as the (urinary bladder, the gall bladder and the stomach) of the leg. You might be wondering what is san Jiao. It is the only meridian from the other meridians that is not linked to a known human organ. It is by far the most powerful energy pathway for the body metabolism function that is also the triple burner mentioned previously. That upper burner relates organs in the thorax and the breathing function.

Remember you learn earlier that the meridians serve as a tunnel that channels your body energy flow following a roadmap to continuously provide energy to your whole body in a mechanical way. Picturing a sophisticated system with a route, there must be some point where all the different meridians meet as a point of intersection. Let's call them traffic red lights or connecting cables. So, during the flow of energy, there are points of intersection with red lights where the energy could stop when there are blockages within your meridians system of flow. Obviously, there are twelve primary roads in concordance with the twelve organs that the meridians are linked to if we consider each organ as a road or a boulevard. Now, along the road built with boulevards, there are traffic lights that are considered in the ancient knowledge as acupressure points. Considering the substitution as the traffic lights within your body at each intersection, we have 365 traffic lights in total that of course represent the number of acupressure that you have within your body throughout your meridians system. Simply retain here that acupressure points are your body traffic lights inside your body and they are 365 of them. Just like the pulse and the tongue are the two GPS of a person's health conveying his/ her current state of health status and balance, meridians system convey also the person's current state of energy flowing within. I guarantee you that the human body in all its aspect is magic, sophisticated and fully matured to suit its environment.

When the energy within your body is blocked, stagnant or imbalanced within its own system, you as the individual become at higher risk to get sick, stressed, uncomfortable, constipated, physically unbalanced, mentally exhausted, spiritually unsecured, dysfunctional digestive system, lack of energy, fatigue, emotionally unstable etc. A blockage in a meridian causes definitely an interruption, a disruption in the flow of energy. That same blocked energy will then have to find another to continue its route; usually rerouting itself through other meridians that leads to a buildup of energy on one side of the blockage and a deficiency of energy on the other. This situation creates what we call an imbalance of energy. And when there exist an imbalance of energy within the meridian system, there are health issues that can be caused as a consequence. That's why you are hearing the term "balance your energy".

The good news is that your energy flow does not have to necessarily stop at the red lights to jeopardize your health. Your body energy flow can continuously flow freely with no blockages at all. And it is actually the intention of the maker of mankind. The red lights are there simply to warn us of something in your life-style that is not lining up with the proper and intended way of living. I have covered paragraphs throughout this book or my other books on what our body, mind and soul require and need for healthy life on our journey in this planet; a list that is not exhaustive. The key is to keep your meridians lines open without any stop that will in turn balance each organ that correspond to each meridian thereby restoring or keeping their ability to continue functioning properly, doing the job they were each assigned to do.

In a case of blockage, you can do exercise, stretching, breathing control, tai chi, rotation postures, acupressure work, massages, self-massage, yoga, stretching-bending-flexing, some traditional dance techniques, meditation and all other techniques I have covered throughout this book and do your own deeper research to learn more about each meridian and its organ specific function to prevent diseases.

Born on Earth as a Teacher and a Student

We are living nowadays in this 21srt century a world wide spread of marketing and commercials influencing the way the majority of people think, buy or spend their energy instead of focusing in their priorities and what they alone have the power to change. We must be reminded including myself that there are a lot of things that will happen in our lives that we alone cannot change. Some things and events in our lives do not necessarily have to be immediately solved by us or others either. Life is a school that needs to be learned. In this school of life, only you are your own teacher and your own student at the same time. As a teacher, you teach yourself and as a student, you learn from yourself. The inputs of others are merely for your personal library only when you decide to incorporate their inputs or cancel them at the moment. But since we are also students in this life, sometimes we also need more time to digest all the information we acquired from others and from us also.

A primordial life lesson mostly in all walk of life is to try your best not trying to be something that you cannot be. If you try to be something other than yourself, which so many of us get caught up, it will stalk your own natural progress every day, everywhere you go and everything that you will see. Consider an instant the amount of personal pain that you will be inflicting yourself every day of life forcing the impossible and most likely the illusion of the fulfillment once that goal were to be achieved. In this situation, stress and depression might become your companion daily; and you are aware by now that any constant upset over your body will negatively affect your health as your mind is relatively connected to your body. The key is to set yourself some realistic goals and stop trying to be or look like somebody else as the guava tree is not hoping to produce apple fruits nor to grow and look like an apple tree. Be you, be honest to your own self and don't pretend or attempt to be something you are not and probably will not be. Respect yourself enough and start enjoying life as who you are and stop suffering needlessly over something that may be unobtainable. And when you have to necessarily suffer, it has to be over things that are really important, needed and among your set of priorities. And if you wish to change the world or have an impact with what you do, start with your immediate people that you can reach first.

Every Baby is Born with Blue Eyes First

You probably wondered before why your black baby was born with blue eyes first and later changed their color as time went by. Babies are born like that because the iris in their eyes has not yet started creating melanin. The iris is a thin circular structure enveloping the pupil and somewhat controls the amount of light entering the eye. The iris is also responsible for creating melanin and melanin is a pigment that provides color to the eye, to the skin and hair. So with the iris forming melanin later after birth, your baby eyes will change from blue to brown, gray, green, or remain blue depending on how much melanin your iris is able to produce. Brown eyes are due to high level of melanin formation by the iris. It is proven scientifically that we have a dark and black melanin as well as yellow melanin; and that green eyes for example are the mixing of low level of dark melanin and high level of yellow melanin. About three to five percent of the world's population has gray eyes; and people that have gray eyes have little to no melanin in their irises. Blue eyes are known to have started recently, about 6000 to 10000 years ago. Blue eyes happened due to a mutation of genes and the genes that mutated are now interfering with the body's original ability to produce melanin in the iris of the eye. Understand here that melanin is very important for the protection of the eye. Retain here that Melanin protects your eye from the sun light and a person's genes determine for a fact how much melanin they possess in his/her iris. At the end, when you remove melanin from any eye regardless of the eye color or race, it automatically becomes blue, making melanin the important pigment for the changing of the eye color. A higher level of melanin will then mean a better eye protection from the harmful sun light.

For your information purposes, it is proven that people that are left handed also have a left eye dominant and a left brain dominant. And those right handed people have a right eye dominant and a right brain dominant as well.

The eye is actually when paid attention, the most used of all our five senses. Almost everything we do, we need our eye constantly for our information. The eye sees first and transforms whatever seen into an information for our appreciation. I guess that's why it is said that "the eye is the window of the soul".

Conclusion

What does it mean to you when you hear these words "your body is a temple and you shall take good care of it?" Well you can take care of the temple through cleansing, detox, meditation, mental detox, aura cleansing, eating healthy, thinking positive, letting go of the ego and the list goes on. Now if you want to think positive, you must first control your emotions, your feelings and your intentions. And you will not be able to control any emotions without first being able to distinguish them and knowing the reasons why you should do such. Your sense of awareness must first increase.

Use knowledge to change your moods and vibrations. Taking care of your temple is not just a mere statement; it is the beginning and the end. It involves a know-how and practice. The simple fact is, if you don't know the vitamins and minerals required for your temple, how effectively are you really taking care of your temple? How would you take care of your temple when you don't know which food to avoid and which ones to eat? How would you take care of your temple if you have not practiced self-control in thoughts, emotions, feelings, and in deeds? How well are you taking care of your temple if you don't know how to manage your stress, desires and wishes?

The temple is the place God dwells. In order for God to dwell in your temple, you must first cleanse and dust off your temple physically, mentally and spiritually; and none of that will be possible without knowledge. It is said that God is already within you, but it is still your duty to bright God out. You will not be able to pretend your way to the kingdom. You must put in some real work and discipline by practicing the way. There are no short cuts, and singing and dancing aren't going to cut it. Don't be fooled again to think that all you need to do is to believe and praise God when in truth payers or praises are not adding anything into God or taking anything out. The masters point to the way and never asked to be worshiped. Instead they all advised you to let go of your past, worries and stress by learning how to forgive through being present, mindful at all times. They are warning you again to stop worshiping the way and head to the destination instead. Entertain good relationship with yourself and your community.

Choose your partner (wife/husband) wisely and intelligently because your long term health depends also on the stability and peace during your relationship/ marriage. Remember that Light is order and darkness is chaos/disorder. Hopefully, you are ready to cohabit with robots now because artificial intelligence (AI) is on its way to becoming the new normal. When in doubt of who you are, think of the human race as one member/ branch from the same tree. All skin color other than black is actually a discoloration due to different weathers and genes mutations through time, subsequently making everyone originated from the same ancestors with an original Black Skin. Pandemics like the one we are having in 2020 (corona virus) also run their own cycles just like any other calamities. Hundred years ago in 1918, we had the influenza pandemic commonly known as the Spanish flu that killed more than 50 million people worldwide. That's one of the reasons you must teach the Law to keep yours safe.

The events from the universe repeat themselves time after time just like your own personal life events. The laws apply to everyone including the greater beings, the planets and remain unapologetic and there is no-one nowhere upstairs forgiving you for transgressing them. That would break the law of cause and effect that applies to the whole universe including you; right? Isn't it why karma exists; that you shall reap what you sow? If you jump from the top of a high rise building with no jumpsuit, should you be surprised that you will not defy gravity and break your neck? At the end, the Law remains the Law. Your job is to pay attention to the Spirit; its signs and the different omens surrounding your life and activities. Thrive for the Light and your soul will be called. The statement in the Bible that says that "the Church shall never be overcome" is actually "The chosen ones shall never be overcome". And there were no churches before the creation of Christianity; it was called Temples which itself is an English translation.

Laws of the lands change and it is therefore not to be relied on naively because illogical and immoral laws could be legalized even though against the principles of life. Slavery was legal in some cultures but immoral. Focus only on getting yourself and yours ready to cross over any obstacle at your path, because even the birds build their own nest without whining nor relying on some supernatural interventions. It is time for you to learn how to save yourself instead of looking out desperately for one savior. No-one is neither motherless nor fatherless in this universe and no-one is neither favored nor disfavored; everyone must reach the highest consciousness by himself to be saved from the laws.

UNTIL NEXT TIME, KEEP READING AND WRITING, AHMED OUT.

Biography

- The Emerald Tablets of Thoth
- The Kybalion
- Looking After your Body – An Owner's Guide to Successful Aging, Reader's Digest
- Your Future Together – 2009 California Department of Public health
- The Seven Souls of Man and their Culmination in Christ –Gerald Massey 1900's
- Jesus the Egyptian –Richard A. Gabriel
- Christ in Egypt: The Horus-Jesus Connection –D.M. Murdock/Acharya S.
- The Egyptian Star of Bethlehem –Robert G. Bauval (excerpted from Secret Chamber)
- Ahmed Y. Tatieta (2017) Soul Pathway to Total Health
- John Gordon (2004) Egypt, Child of Atlantis: a Radical Interpretation of the Origins of Civilization
- Carolyn Collins Petersen (2013) Astronomy 101
- Chuck Missler (1999) Cosmic Codes; Hidden Messages from the Edge of Eternity.

- A. C. Bhaktivedanta Swami Prabhupada (2004) Bhakti-Yoga; The Art of Eternal Love
- Dan Brown (2009) *The Lost Symbol*
- Robert C. Atkins, M.D. (2002) Dr. Atkins' New Diet Revolution
- Dr. Les Parrott (2003) Shoulda Coulda Woulda: Live in the Present/ Find Your Future
- Marcus Aurelius (175 CE. Printed 2017) Meditations
- L. Mike Henry/ K. Sean Harris (2002) Jamaican Herbs & Medicinal Plants and their Uses
- Betty R. Price (1982) Through the Fire & Through the Water: My triumph Over Cancer
- Pema Chodron (2013) How to Meditate – A Practical Guide to Making Friends with your Mind
- Astral Books (2010) The Evil Eye – Protect yourself against the terrors of the Evil Eye.
- Holy Bible (King James Version)
- Quran
- A. C. Bhaktivedanta Swami Prabhupada (1972, 1983) Bhagavad Gita – As It Is
- L. Ron Hubbard (2007) Scientology- A New Slant on Life
- Stefan Chmelik (1999) Chinese Herbal Secrets (the key to total health)
- Denise Whichello Brown & Sandra White (2001) Alternative Health Therapies (the complete guide to aromatherapy, massage and reflexology)

- Barron's (2nd Edition 2004) Anatomy and Physiology (the easy way)
- Paula R. Hartz (1993) Taoism (world religion)
- Theresa Cheung (2006) The Elements Encyclopedia of the Psychic World (the Ultimate a-z of Spirits, mysteries and the paranormal)
- Satguru Sivaya Subramuniyaswami (1993) Dancing With Siva (Hinduism's contemporary catechism)
- Michael Philips (2008) The Undercover Philosopher
- Osho (2004) Buddha (his life and teachings)
- Christmas Humphreys (1962) Zen – A Way of Life
- Kendra Sims (2018) I'm Saved But I Struggle (a realistic view of salvation)
- Eckhart Tolle (2008) A New Earth (Awakening to Your Life's Purpose)
- Deepak Chopra (2004) The Book of Secrets (Unlocking the Hidden Dimensions of Your Life)
- Leo Tolstoy (1998) A Calendar of Wisdom (Daily Thoughts to Nourish the Soul)
- Ernesto Ortiz, LMT, CST (2009) Hot Stone Massage Therapy (A Guide to the Total Mind-Body Experience)
- Deborah Mitchell; Foreword by Hunter Yost, M.D. (2009) The Complete Book of Nutritional Healing
- Gaby Dun (2019) Bad With Money (The Imperfect Art of Getting your Financial Shit Together)
- Ahmed Tatieta (2020) The Path to a long and Healthy Life

- Mayo Clinic (2014) The Essential Diabetes Book (How to Prevent, Control, and Live Well with Diabetes)
- Hippolytus, Refutatio Omnium – Haeresium vii
- Aristotle, fr 591 (ed. V. Rose)
- Argonautica IV. 264
- Plutarch, Moralia, transl. by F. C. Babbit, sect. 76
- Lucian, Astrology, transl. by A.M. Harmon (1936), P.367, par. 26
- The Nihongi Chronicles of Japan (I.ii, in transactions and proceedings of the Japanese society, Vol. I (1896) which recount how "heaven and earth … produced the moon-god."
- Phyllis A. Balch, CNC (2002) "Prescription for Herbal Healing- An Easy-to-Use A-to-Z Reference to Hundreds of Common Disorders and Their Herbal Remedies "

www.ingramcontent.com/pod-product-compliance
Lightning Source LLC
LaVergne TN
LVHW090934080826
845145LV00003B/748

* 9 7 8 1 7 3 4 6 7 7 3 8 6 *